COVID VACCINE

ISSUES AND CHALLANGES

DR. MUKTA GOYAL MR. KRITTIBAS DUTTA

ISBN 979-888569178-9

Our parents, family members, and friends who instilled in us the values of love, care, humility, and gentleness

Contents

Preface

The coronavirus disease, Covid 19, as a pandemic shook the world health care system and economy to such an extent that the epidemic is still spreading and showing no signs of decreasing trend. In these conditions more and more vaccination is the only way to fight the Covid 19 various. India is considered the world's vaccine manufacturing hub. This contributes 60 percent to the global vaccine supply. The country has the potential to produce three billion coronavirus disease 2019 (Covid-19) vaccine doses annually. India exported Excel to more than 90 countries.

As India rolled out one of the world's biggest inoculation programs, some health care workers and frontline workers were hesitating because of safety. When most of the world was struggling to get vaccines for inoculation, India had the opposite problem, 'Plenty of shots, but a shortage of people to take them. Vaccine hesitancy among the Indian population is prevailing even now. Unless, the inoculation rate increases, India will fall short of its target of inoculating people to its mark.

Our central and states government are trying their best to the vaccination process in India with government machinery. As a third-world country, India has faced many challenges to vaccination among the largest population. Our nation has overcome the first two variants of coronavirus with vaccination and corona awareness instructions. The "Precautionary Dose" was announced by Prime Minister Narendra Modi last month amid continued demands for booster doses in view of the Omicron threat.

This work is possible with the blessing of our parents and family members whose continued inspiration guided us for publications this book in time. Our sincere thanks to all the chapter contributors without their contributions this edited volume would not have been possible. As a whole, the book got the complete shape because of the great initiative of ABS publication. We would like to express our thanks to all the parts of the publishing house. Finally, I do hereby declare that the chapter contributed by the contributors are of their own views; if any discrepancies or legal issues arising out of this publication the contributors will be responsible for this; the editors or publishers will not bear the responsibility.

Dr. Mukta Goyal
Mr. Krittibas Datta

CHAPTER ONE

History of Vaccine in India

Introduction

Vaccination is a proven and cost-effective intervention for child survival1. Every country in the world must have an immunization program in place to deliver specific vaccines to targeted beneficiaries, with a particular emphasis on pregnant women, infants, and children, who are at a high risk of diseases preventable by vaccines. There are at least 27 causative agents against which vaccines are available, and many more are being developed.

Vaccine

A vaccine is a biological preparation that improves immunity to a particular disease. A vaccine is an Immuno-biological substance designed to produce specific protection against the given disease. A vaccine is "antigenic" but not "pathogenic"

A vaccine typically contains an agent that resembles a disease-causing microorganism and is often made from a weakened or killed form of the microbes.

The agent stimulates the body's immune system to recognize the agent as foreign and destroy it and keep a record of it. So that the immune system can more easily recognize and destroy any of these microorganisms that it later encounters.

The word vaccine was first used by Edward Jenner in 1796. The word vaccine was derived from a Latin word Vacca-Cow. The terms vaccine and vaccination are derived from Variolae Vaccine (small Pox of the Cow). The term was devised by Edward Jenner to denote Cowpox. He firstly cured the disease smallpox through his self-made vaccine.

History

Vaccines and vaccination have a long history, dating back to the first attempts in society to prevent disease. Smallpox (along with many other infectious diseases such as measles) has been known since ancient times and is thought to have originated in India or Egypt over 3,000 years ago. Many learned minds and physicians, including Thucydides in 430 BC and Rhazes (also known as Abu Bakr) in 910 AD, observed that people infected with smallpox were protected from future infections.

In 900 AD, Abu Bakr also provided the first (and most likely the only) account of distinguishing between measles and smallpox. There are few descriptions of disease occurrences from India; however, one of the best-documented smallpox epidemics was reported from Goa in 1545 AD, when an estimated 8,000 children died. Smallpox has been referred to as the "Indian Plague" by historians and physicians, implying that the disease was once widespread in India. Smallpox is referred to as the 'Indian Plague,' implying that the disease was once widespread in India.

Evidence suggests that smallpox inoculation was practiced in China around 1000 AD, as well as India, Turkey, and possibly Africa.

Smallpox affected all races and regions of the world, causing frequent epidemics, and inoculation was practiced in a number of East Asian countries; however, the practice did not reach Europe, particularly the United Kingdom, until the early 18th century12. Given the severity of the disease, various approaches to preventing it were tried. In 1774, Benjamin Jesty, an English farmer and cattle-breeder, experimented on his wife and two children with cowpox matter inoculation and nearly discovered the first smallpox vaccine.

During the late 1760s while serving his apprenticeship as a surgeon Edward Jenner learned the story common the rural areas that dairy workers would never have the often-fatal or disfiguring disease smallpox because they had already had cowpox which has a very mild effect in humans.

In 1796 Jenner took the Pus from the hand of a milkmaid with cowpox, scratched it into the arm of an 8-year-old boy. Six weeks later inoculated the boy with smallpox, afterward observing that he did not catch smallpox. Jenner extended his studies and in 1798 reported that his vaccine was safe in children and adults. In 1798, Jenner published his seminal work titled 'An enquiry into the causes and effects of Variolae Vaccinae.' Smallpox vaccination spread quickly after Jenner's publication, particularly in Europe and America. The smallpox vaccine arrived in India in 1802 (within four years).

The second generation of the vaccine was introduced in the 1880s by Louis Pasteur who developed vaccine for chicken cholera and anthrax.

From the late nineteenth centuries, vaccines were considered as a matter of national Prestige and compulsory vaccination laws were passed.

Vaccination

Vaccination is the administration of antigen material to stimulate the immune system of an individual to develop adaptive immunity to a disease.

Vaccination is a method of giving antigen to stimulate the immune response through active Immunization.

In May 1802, the first doses of smallpox vaccine lymph arrived in India. On June 14, 18026, Anna Dusthall, a three-year-old child from Bombay (now Mumbai), became the first person in India to receive smallpox vaccine. The smallpox vaccine as lymph was sent from Bombay to Madras, Poona (Pune), Hyderabad, and Surat via a human chain of vaccinees. Because of the proven benefits of smallpox vaccination, variolation was outlawed in many European countries and in some Indian provinces as early as 1804. Officials from the Indian Medical Services made special efforts to spread the word about smallpox vaccination.

Immunity

Immunity is the ability of the body to defend itself from 'foreign bodies. This means rejecting infections, clearing up dust that gets in the lungs and killing cancer cells. Immunity is of two types. Innate immunity protects the host against infection but has no 'memory', and so gives no long-term immunity.

- **Innate Immunity**: We are all born with some level of immunity to invaders.
- **Adaptive (acquired) Immunity**: This protects from pathogens that develops as we go through life.
- **Passive Immunity**: Immunity conferred by an antibody produced in another host. It may be acquired naturally or artificially (through an antibody-containing preparation). This type of immunity is "borrowed" from another source, but it does not last indefinitely.
- **Active Immunity:** Resistance developed in response to the stimulus by an antigen (infecting agent or vaccine) and is characterized by the production of antibodies by the host.

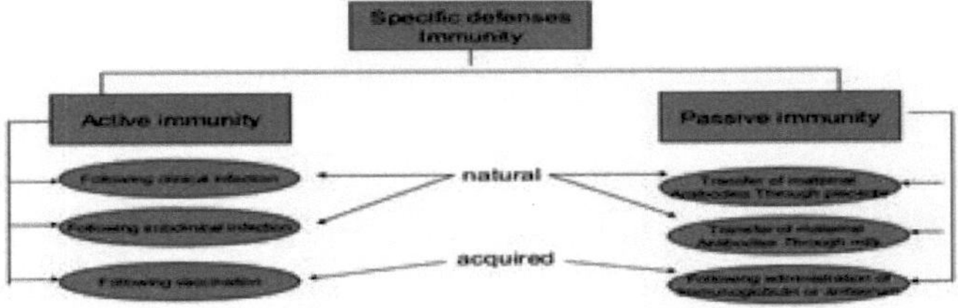

Immunity

Immunization

Immunization is a way of preventing a person from getting a disease. This is done by making the person's body come into contact with a bit of the disease so that the body learns how to fight it. The body's ability to fight off disease is called its immune system. The material is known as an immunogen.

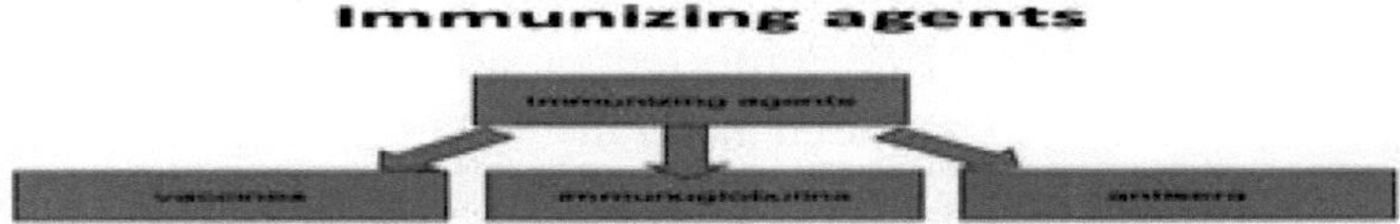

Immunizing agents

Immunoglubulins

There are five major classes IgM, IgA,IgG,IgE, IgD. Two types of immunoglobulins preparations are available for Passive immunization

- Normal Human Immunogloubins
- Specific (hyper immune) Human Immunogloubins

Antisera

These are materials prepared in animals or non human sources such as Horses.

History of COVID Vaccine in India

The COVID-19 pandemic in India is part of the global coronavirus disease 2019 (COVID-19) pandemic caused by the severe acute respiratory syndrome coronavirus (SARS-CoV-2). According to official figures as of September 27, 2021, India has the world's second-highest number of confirmed cases (after the United States of America) with 33,678,786 reported cases of COVID-19 infection and the third-highest number of COVID-19 deaths (after the United States and Brazil) with 466,147 deaths. However, these figures show significant under-reporting. The Government of India confirmed India's first case of Coronavirus disease 2019 on 30 January 2020 in the state of Kerala, when a university student from Wuhan travelled back to the state and since then "Coronavirus" terminology is known to us.

On January 16, 2021, India began administering COVID-19 vaccines. As of November 22, 2021, India had administered over 1.17 billion doses in total, including the first and second doses of currently approved vaccines. In India, nearly half of the eligible population received at least one shot, and 19% received both doses within the first nine months of vaccine availability.

The Oxford–AstraZeneca vaccine (manufactured under license by Serum Institute of India under the trade name Covishield) and Covaxin were initially approved in India (a vaccine developed locally by Bharat Biotech). They have since been joined by the Sputnik V (manufactured under licence by Dr. Reddy's Laboratories, with additional production from Serum Institute of India beginning in September, Moderna vaccines, Johnson & Johnson vaccine, and ZyCoV-D (a vaccine developed locally by Zydus Cadila), as well as other vaccine candidates undergoing local clinical trials.

Vaccine Development and Distribution

As of early May 2020, India had over 30 vaccine candidates in development, with many already in pre-clinical trials. The Serum Institute of India (SII) in Pune is the world's largest vaccine manufacturer. Because of this existing capacity, India was able to become a major participant in the

COVAX programme, which distributes vaccines to developing countries. SII began animal trials of vaccine candidates in February 2020. SII announced in April 2020 that it would apply to the Drug Controller General of India (DCGI) for clinical trials. SII president Adar Poonawalla predicted that a vaccine would be available within a year, with an efficacy of 70 to 80 percent.

SII received approvals for phase 2 and phase 3 trials of its version of a vaccine developed by AstraZeneca and the University of Oxford's Vaccitech in August 2020. SII collaborated with GAVI and the Bill and Melinda Gates Foundation to produce 100 million doses of vaccine for developing countries. The SII intended to produce 1.5 to 2.5 billion doses of the AstraZeneca vaccine each year under the brand name "Covishield." By the time it received approval in January 2021, the company had accumulated 50 million doses, falling far short of its own target of 400 million.

Hyderabad-based Bharat Biotech, in collaboration with FluGen in the United States, expects to begin clinical trials for a nasal vaccine in late 2020. In May 2020, the Indian Council of Medical Research partnered with Bharat Biotech to develop a COVID vaccine entirely in India. It received DCGI approval in June 2020 to begin phase 1 and phase 2 trials on its vaccine, BBV152 (trade name "Covaxin"). Covaxin was able to build immunity in pre-clinical trials on animals, according to a report published in September 2020. Covaxin's production capacity has been increased to 700 million doses per year.

Cadila Healthcare began developing vaccines, including a viral vector vaccine and a DNA plasmid vaccine, in March 2020. Cadila conducted early human trials of its vaccine candidate ZyCoV-D in mid-July 2020, and received approval for phase 3 trials in January 2021. Cadila expects to receive emergency authorization between May and June 2021, with large-scale production beginning in April 2021. Cadila Healthcare reported 66.6 percent efficacy against symptomatic COVID-19 and 100 percent efficacy against moderate or severe disease in its interim analysis of phase 3 trial data on July 1, 2021.

Dr. Reddy's partnered with the Russian Direct Investment Fund (RDIF) in September 2020 to conduct phase 3 trials of the Sputnik V vaccine in India and to distribute the vaccine once approved. In April 2021, RDIF CEO Kirill Dmitriev told NDTV that the vaccine would be manufactured by "five great manufacturers in India," and that the country could become Sputnik V's "production hub" for use and export. Dr. Reddy's is also collaborating with the RDIF on the approval of "Sputnik Light," a Sputnik V regimen consisting only of the first dose.

The DCGI removed the requirement for India-specific clinical trials (bridging trials) for vaccine candidates developed outside of India on 2 June 2021, provided they have already been approved by a recognised international public health agency such as the World Health Organization (WHO), European Medicines Agency (EMA), US Food and Drug Administration (FDA), UK Medicines and Healthcare products Regulatory Agency (MHRA), or Japan's Pharmaceuticals and Medical Development Agency (PMDA). These modifications were made to help speed up the availability of vaccines that are already in use in other countries.

It was reported in mid-July that approval of the Moderna and Pfizer vaccines, as well as a shipment of vaccines donated by the US (including the AstraZeneca, Janssen, Moderna, and Pfizer vaccines), had been delayed due to requests from their manufacturers for indemnity clauses from Indian authorities, which would relieve them of legal liability for adverse reactions.

The Indian government announced on September 21, 2021, that it will not purchase the Pfizer-BioNTech and Moderna vaccines because domestic production of more affordable and easier-to-store vaccines has increased.

Prime Minister Narendra Modi announced at the Quad summit that India would make 8 million doses of the J&J vaccine available by the end of October as part of the Quad vaccine partnership. The Biological E will manufacture it in India. This would be ready by the end of October, which would be consistent with our decision to resume vaccine export.

In January 2021, India launched Vaccine Maitri (vaccine friendship), a humanitarian initiative aimed at leveraging the country's pharmaceutical industry to export Indian-made vaccines to other countries. According to the Ministry of External Affairs, India has donated over 5.5 million vaccines to neighbouring countries such as Bahrain, Bangladesh, Bhutan, Maldives, Mauritius, Myanmar, Nepal, Seychelles, and Sri Lanka since 20 January, and the country also plans to send doses to Africa, Nicaragua, Oman, the Caribbean Community, and the COVAX programme, as well as distribute vaccines to other countries through commercial exports.

As of 10 March 2021, India had distributed over 58 million vaccine doses to 65 nations via the scheme, but due to India's domestic need for vaccines, these exports were suspended later in March, and the suspension was expected to last the rest of the year.

Conclusions

The evolution of vaccination efforts in India is far more complex than presented in this chapter, and each event deserves a thorough examination. Though disease prevention efforts were undertaken in India, vaccination has been met with reluctance, opposition, and slow acceptance throughout its history. Due to operational challenges, coverage in the country remains inequitable. The lessons learned from previous events have been analysed and interpreted in order to guide immunisation efforts. There are numerous historical lessons to be learned from extending the benefits of immunisation to every possible beneficiary in the country in order to achieve the stated policy goals.

References

- Fenner F, Henderson DA, Arita I, Jezek Z, Ladnyi ID. *Smallpox and its eradication*. Geneva: World Health Organization; 1988. p. 369-71.
- Basu RN, Jezek Z, Ward NA. *The eradication of smallpox from India.* New Delhi, India: World Health Organization, South-East Asia Regional Office; 1979.
- Bhattacharya S, Harrison M, Worboys M. *Fractured states: Smallpox, public health and vaccination policy in British India, 1800-1947.* Hyderabad: Orient Longman; 2006.
- Bazin H. *The eradication of smallpox: Edward Jenner and the first and only eradication of a human infectious disease*. San Diego: Academic Press; 2000.
- Brimnes N. Variolation, vaccination and popular resistance in early colonial south India. *Med Hist* 2004; *48* : 199-228.
- Dowdle WR. The principles of disease elimination and eradication. *Bull World Health Organ* 1998; *76* (Suppl 2):
- 22-5.
- Fitchett JR, Heymann DL. Smallpox vaccination and opposition by anti-vaccination societies in 19th century Britain. *Hist Med* 1995; *2* : E17.
- Wujastyk D. A pious fraud: the Indian claims for pre-Jennerian smallpox vaccination. In: Jan Meulenbeld G, Wujastyk D, editors. *Studies on Indian medical history*. Delhi: Motilal Banarsidass Publishers; 2001. p. 121-54.
- Chandrakant Lahariya, A brief history of vaccines & vaccination in India, Indian J Med Res 139, April 2014, pp 491-511
- https://en.wikipedia.org/wiki/COVID-19_vaccination_in_India.

CHAPTER TWO

COVID-19 vaccination Process and Policies in India

Introduction

We all are well known that we are going now in a critical socio conditions duo to COVID -19. Every sector of a human being is affected by this viral disease for the last two years. Every level of medical sciences referred to vaccination as the key way to human safety against the COVID -19 viruses. Scientists have tried to make vaccines to fight the coronavirus for saving humans across the world from the first phase of COVID-19. In this regard, many state and private institutes have made vaccine against COVID-19 virus in different names and dose. In an attempt to control the COVID-19 pandemic, India initially authorized the emergency use of two vaccines, each requiring two doses – Covishield developed by Oxford/AstraZeneca and Covaxin developed by Bharat Biotech in collaboration with the Indian Council for Medical Research (ICMR) and the National Institute of Virology The vaccination drive in India started on January 16, 2021, with an ultimate target of vaccinating 300 million people by August 2021.

Our central and states government are trying their best to the vaccination process in India with government machinery. As a third-world country, India has faced many challenges to vaccination among the largest population. Our nation has overcome the first two variants of coronavirus with vaccination and corona awareness instructions. Our vaccination process is facing a new challenge. Here we discuss the issues and challenges facing COVID-19 vaccination in India.

Vaccination Process in India against COVID-19

Almost a year after India reported its first case, on 16 January, India launched the largest vaccine drive, starting its journey on the road to recovery from a pandemic. Manish Kumar, a 34-year-old sanitation worker at Delhi's All India Institute of Medical Sciences (AIIMS), became the first person in India to receive the COVID-19 vaccine. The Ministry of Health and Family Welfare have a three phased approach for the vaccine roll-out that will see health workers vaccinated first, followed by frontline and essential workers and then people over 50 years and those with comorbidities. After months of planning, including numerous dry runs to iron out any concerns, there was renewed optimism and energy when the first COVID-19 vaccine was administered.

The first phase of vaccine roll-out prioritized 30 million health care and frontline workers. Vaccine rollout however has been slower than expected and the country is now facing shortages due to an inadequate scale-up of vaccine production so far.

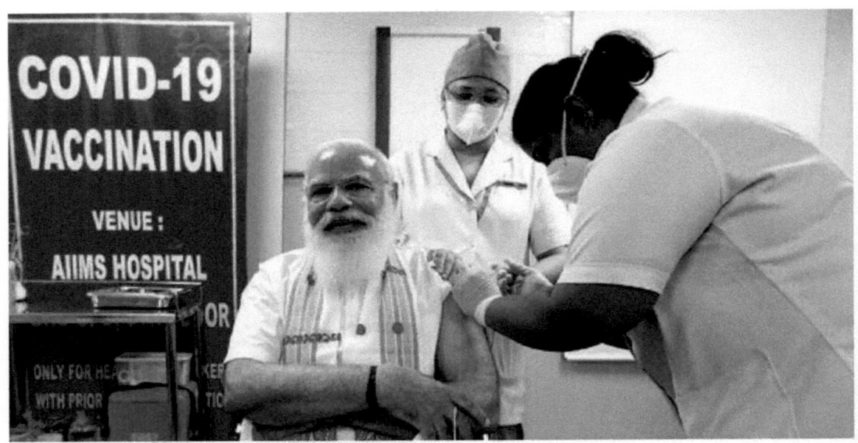

Source: nytimes.com

Normally there are four steps for the COVID19 vaccine of any eligible persons in India. The first step is waiting for a security check to enter the vaccination center. The Second step is online verification and ID check of a person in the vaccination center. The next step is vaccine pushing in the human body by the health worker. The last step is 30 minutes observation of the vaccinated person under the health worker in the particular vaccination center.

Steps for COVID19 vaccine

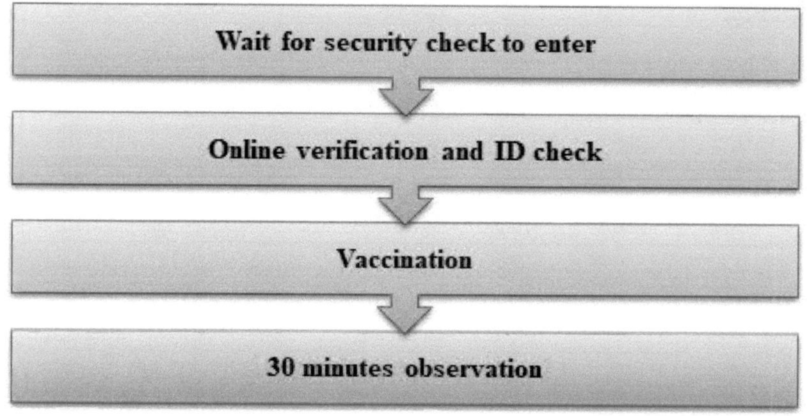

Steps for COVID19 vaccine

In the starting point, India aimed to immunize the following people in a phased manner. Health Care Workers (HCWs) and Front Line Workers (FLWs), followed by citizens more than 45 years of age and eventually citizens more than 18 years of age. This requires registration on a digital platform called COVID-19 Vaccine Intelligence Network (Co-WIN), after which information of the vaccination site to visit and time will be shared with the beneficiary. The number of individuals who receive vaccine doses is tracked on this system.

COVID-19 vaccination dose in India: India has delivered over a billion vaccine doses, making it the second-highest dispenser of COVID-19 vaccines globally but the gap between the proportion of the population that has got at least one dose and two doses is widest in India. The key factor responsible for this, according to experts, is the gap between two doses of Covishield which comprises 88% of the administered vaccines in India. The spacing of 12-16 weeks is among the longest in the world. As per our government recommendation, the 2nd dose of COVAXIN should be administered in the interval of 4 to 6 weeks from the date of 1st dose administration. For COVISHIELD the recommended interval is 4 to 8 weeks while an interval of 6 to 8 weeks gives enhanced protection. You may choose the date of 2nd dose vaccination as per your convenience.

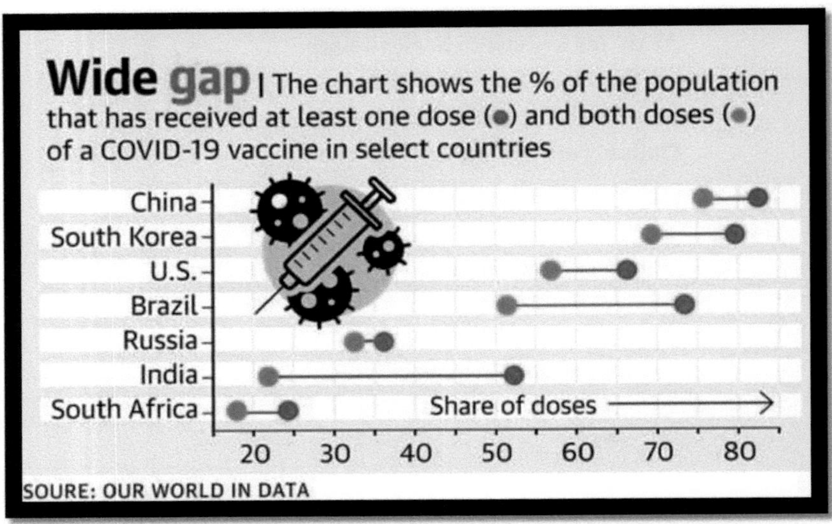

Source: thehindu.com

The "precautionary dose" was announced by Prime Minister Narendra Modi last month amid continued demands for booster doses in view of the Omicron threat. Those eligible for booster shots will, however, get them only 9 months after receiving the second dose of the Covid vaccine. Those above the age of 60 years who have co-morbidities like diabetes, hypertension, and other chronic ailments have the option of getting the "Precaution Dose" on the advice of their doctor. On the other hand "Corona warriors, healthcare, and frontline workers have a huge contribution in keeping the country safe. Therefore, from the point of view of precaution, the government has decided to start administering "Precaution Doses" for healthcare and frontline workers,"

Vaccinated graph in India and comparatively World

Vaccinated Lavel	INDIA	WORLD
Total doses given	152Cr	937Cr
Fully vaccinated	63.2Cr	392Cr
%fully vaccinated	45.8%	50.3%

Source: *Data retrieve on 10.01.2021 from website, Government of India*

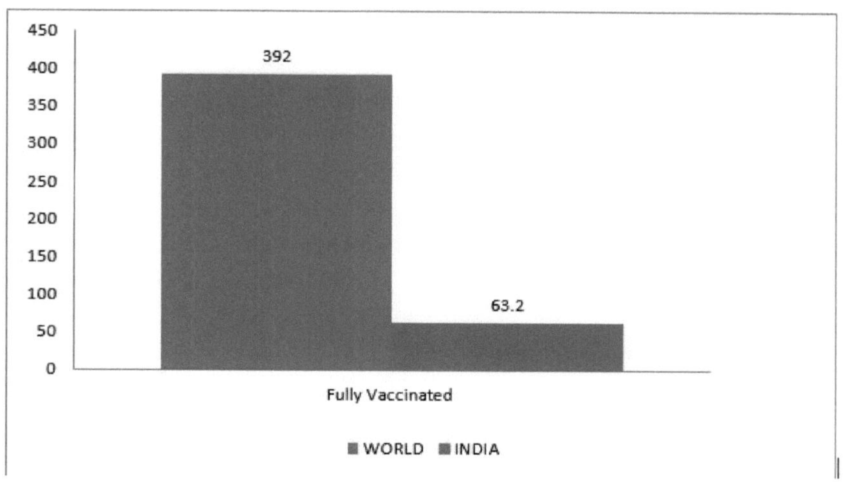

Source: *Data retrieved on 10.01.2021 from the website, Government of India*

As per the above-mentioned table and graph (63.2Cr) 45.8% population of India has fully vaccinated and 152Cr population has taken the COVID vaccine dose. Comparably (392Cr) 50.3% population has been vaccinated all over the World and the total COVID vaccine dose is given 937Cr.

Vaccination challenges in India against COVID-19: India has the potential to produce 60% of the vaccine stock in the world. The Government of India plans to inoculate around 300 million individuals of the priority group in the initial phase, in this regard problems to equitable distribution. According to the government report, 895 million accounts for 65.5% of the total population living in a rural area. The ultimate goal should be to ensure that this vaccination drive is accessible to these rural populations, many of whom reside in remote villages and are often neglected. Besides the Indian vaccination process are facing many challenges or gap, the important challenge are mentioned below:

a. **Manufacturing Challenges:** The Covishield vaccine, manufactured by the Pune-based Serum Institute of India, accounts for nearly 90% of vaccine doses in India. Covishield is the brand name in India for the Oxford-AstraZeneca vaccine. Covaxin, a vaccine developed in India by Bharat Biotech, has emergency use authorization in India but still has not been able to meet production expectations. Despite the initial vaccine shortages experienced during the second wave, supply lines of vaccines seem to have vastly improved in the past three months.

b. **Vaccine Distribution:** Vaccine distribution is the main challenge in India. The greatest challenge at the moment of dispensing the vaccine to the vast population across the country. Vaccine distribution is extraordinarily difficult to accomplish during a short time. Besides our country has no sufficient storage system for vaccine stores in every corner. With just about 30,000 cold storage facilities scattered across the country, the number is the sine of cold storage shortage. So after the production of vaccine against COVID-19 equal distribution to every corner in the country is impossible.

c. **Lack of Internet Communication:** The authorities have incorporated CO-WIN, a vaccine tracking and registration app to manage, deliver, and track the country's mass vaccination campaign. Eligible citizens can use either the CO-WIN platform or Aarogya Setu, India's COVID-19 contact tracing app, to book their vaccine appointment anytime, anywhere. Integration with Aarogya Setu enables CO-WIN users to download a QR-coded vaccine certificate and stay up-to-date about their COVID-19 risk via contact tracing and self-assessment features. But lack of proper internet penetration across rural communities is a potent hurdle for the vaccination drive.

d. **Price challenge of COVID vaccine:** The majority of countries are not paying from their own pocket for Covid vaccination to the people. In this regards the cost of vaccines in the private market in India is the highest — almost $12 for getting a shot of Covishield and $17 for Covaxin. The cost of vaccines in the private sector has shot up by up to six times from Rs 250. It now ranges from Rs 700-900 for Kovishield manufactured by the Serum Institute of India (SII) and Rs 1,250-1,500 for Covaxin manufactured by Bharat Biotech (BB). it is not easy to pay this amount for the COVID vaccine of all Indians. On the other hand hopeful news is that our Government has provided the vaccine free of cost. But anyone who won't vaccinate from the private sector then pays the fixed amount of the person.

e. **Health worker and infrastructer challenge:** The vaccination drive is incomplete without qualified healthcare personnel. India has 2.9 million registered nursing personnel, translating to a ratio of 1.6 nurses per 1000 population, far below the WHO norms of 3 per 1000 population. Furthermore, the country is also deficient in doctors, at 0.9 per 1000 population (below the norm of 1 per 1000 population). The Indian Government plans to include Auxiliary Nurse Midwives (ANM) working on Universal Immunization Programmes for COVID-19 vaccination purposes.
f. **Lack of awareness:** A large number of people in rural India aren't getting vaccines or tests facility due to lack of awareness COVID 19. But alongside is the massive wall of suspicion, rumors, fake news, and fear driving the hesitation, or plain refusal to both vaccine and testing.

Concluding Observation: After the first and second waves now we are fighting against Omicron a new variant of COVID virus with the help of vaccine and safety protocols. In an attempt to control the COVID-19 pandemic, India initially authorized the emergency use of two vaccines, each requiring two doses – Covishield developed by Oxford/AstraZeneca and Covaxin developed by Bharat Biotech in collaboration with the Indian Council for Medical Research (ICMR) and the National Institute of Virology The vaccination drive in India started on January 16, 2021, with an ultimate target of vaccinating 300 million people by August 2021. The first phase of vaccine roll-out prioritized 30 million health care and frontline workers. India grappled with low rates of both registration and vaccine administration during the initial stages of the vaccination campaign, likely because of vaccine hesitancy, misinformation propagated by social media, and technical glitches in the online registration platform. Moreover, the requirement to register online for receiving vaccines may have contributed to low vaccination rates as more than half of the Indian population does not have access to the internet. We hope that near future our country will be overcome all the barriers and successfully complete the vaccination for the entire citizen.

- Pandey, A., Sah, P., Moghadas, S. M., Mandal, S., Banerjee, S., Hotez, P. J., & Galvani, A. P. (2021). Challenges facing COVID-19 vaccination in India: Lessons from the initial vaccine rollout. *Journal of Global Health*,

11.

- DeRoo, S. S., Pudalov, N. J., & Fu, L. Y. (2020). Planning for a COVID-19 vaccination program. *Jama, 323*(24), 2458-2459.
- Bagcchi, S. (2021). The world's largest COVID-19 vaccination campaign. *The Lancet. Infectious Diseases, 21*(3), 323.
- Chakraborty, C., Sharma, A. R., Bhattacharya, M., Agoramoorthy, G., & Lee, S. S. (2021). The current second wave and COVID-19 vaccination status in India. *Brain, behavior, and immunity, 96*, 1-4.
- Kumar, V. M., Pandi-Perumal, S. R., Trakht, I., & Thyagarajan, S. P. (2021). Strategy for COVID-19 vaccination in India: the country with the second-highest population and number of cases. *npj Vaccines, 6*(1), 1-7.
- Booster Doses For Frontline Workers, Seniors Begins: 10 Points, NDTV, dated on January 10, 2022 (https://www.ndtv.com/india-news/booster-doses-for-frontline-workers-seniors-begin-today-10-facts-2698666)
- https://economictimes.indiatimes.com/opinion/et-commentary/

view-rural-india-desperately-needs-mass-awareness-campaigns-to-snap-out-of-covid-hesitancy/
articleshow/
82613951.cms?utm_source=contentofinterest&utm_medium=text&utm_campaign=cppst

CHAPTER THREE

A Critical Analysis Of Covid-19 Vaccine Hesitancy Among Adolescents

Abstract

The emergence of human Corona virus has thrown the world the midst of new pandemic. Equitable access to safe and effective vaccines is critical to ending the COVID-19 pandemic. The vaccines produce protection against the disease as a result of developing an immune response to the SARS-Cov-2 virus. Developing an immunity through vaccination means there is a reduced risk of developing the illness and its consequences. Health organizations have launched many programmes to increase the uptake of COVID-19 vaccines among people, however, vaccination coverage among adolescents is not as much that of the effort. Adolescents are hesitated to take COVID-19 vaccine. The present study, analyses and explores the various factors that cause vaccine hesitancy among adolescents. A sample of 125 adolescent students, who had not been vaccinated was selected as sample. The survey method was adopted for the study. The findings revealed that Vaccine Hesitancy among adolescents are caused by significant factors.

Keywords: Vaccination, Immunity, COVID-19 vaccines, Vaccine Hesitancy, Adolescents.

Introduction

Vaccines are imperative as they aid in boosting the immunity of the body against specific disclosures. The body's immune system helps protect against infections. A vaccine activates the immune system without making the person sick. A good vaccine will provide suitable and prolonged protection against the disease. The number of doses needed varies from vaccine to vaccine. Vaccines are safe. The vaccines offer life-saving protection against a disease that has killed millions. The benefits of the use far outweigh any risks of side effects.

Vaccination is the cornerstone of an efficient healthcare system. Vaccination had made an important contribution to the decreased incidence of numerous infectious diseases and associated mortality. A vaccinated person is less likely to spread infectious diseases to others. So, people who get vaccinated can help protect those who cannot be vaccinated themselves. This includes babies, children, older people, and people with weak immune systems. These groups benefit from others getting vaccinated because the disease then cannot spread in the community. A high number of vaccinations is required to help create this community immunity. When a high number of people are vaccinated chains of infections are stopped.

The outbreak of Corona Virus disease 2019(COVID-2019) has created a global health crisis that has created a deep impact on the way humans perceive the world. People around the world are currently experiencing an emergency, affecting all societies and it has sent billions of people into lockdown. The Worldwide frantic efforts are on track to curb this pandemic. Now that COVID-19 vaccines have reached billions of people worldwide, the evidence is overwhelming that no matter which one is applied, the vaccines offer life-saving protection against this pandemic disease that has killed millions.

Even though the world shares a collective responsibility in fighting COVID-19 pandemic, some people are still hesitant to take COVID- 19 vaccine. The reluctance of people to receive safe and recommended available vaccines is known as 'Vaccine Hesitancy'. The reasons for COVID-19 vaccine hesitancy remain complex, especially among adolescents.

Adolescence is a time of great and rapid cognitive, psychological, social, emotional and physical changes. These changes result in a more adult-like appearance, an increased ability to think abstractly, a greater need for autonomy and independence, increased social and peer comparison and greater peer affiliation. These changes typically translate into adolescents' desire to participate in and eventually lead their decision-making. Adolescence is a period of life during which peers play a pivotal role in decision-making. The narrative of social influence during adolescence often revolves around risky and maladaptive decisions, research findings support the conception that adolescents are more sensitive to peer influence than children or adults, the developmental processes that underlie this sensitivity remain poorly understood.

Social media platforms spread violating misinformation, video highlights and images on the way that the anti-vaccine movement is feeding into the recent surge of misinformation and disinformation swirling around COVID-19. With the wide availability of smartphones, most of adolescents can now access the internet and social media and the information these online platforms share has a great influence upon their decision-making. It also grants several challenges in the form of misinformation including anti-vaccine messaging and incomplete information as well as inconsistent and complicated scientific information that may be difficult to understand correctly. The research findings (Bagateli et. al,2021) revealed that vaccine hesitancy among adolescents is a top threat to global health in the context of the COVID-19 Pandemic because they are more inclined towards misleading information shared by their peers and by social media.

Need and significance of the study

COVID-19 vaccines are the best way to protect oneself and others. Getting people vaccinated is the only long-term solution to the COVID-19 crisis. Older people and those living with chronic medical conditions such as heart disease and diabetes are more likely to experience severe even fatal cases of COVID-19. If more people receive the coronavirus vaccines more vulnerable people can be safe among others. Research (Cadeddu et.al, 2021) has shown that vaccines help to reduce the risk of getting seriously ill of dying from COVID-19. It reduces the risk of catching or spreading COVID-19. The vaccination protects one from Covid- 19 variants.

Adolescents are so risky in the world. Peers and social media impacts almost all aspects of adolescents' lives. Adolescents hesitate to get vaccinated for COVID-19 for many reasons, from personal views and fears to logistical problems of vaccination. But waiting too long to be vaccinated allows the coronavirus to continue spreading in the community, with new variants. Severe COVID-19 can be very dangerous, the sooner get vaccinated sooner one gets protected. In order to effectively conscientize adolescents towards COVID-19 vaccination, it is necessary to analyse their attitude and to identify the various factors that enforced them to become vaccine-hesitant. The need and significance of the study is hence justified.

Statement of the problem

Adolescents often make risky choices because they are unaware on the potential negative consequences associated with that particular action. Most probably they perceived themselves as invulnerable to Negative consequences. Attitudinal constraints, peer group pressures lead them to make decisions that may put their well-being at risk. COVID-19 vaccines are best hope to end the pandemic. Scientists, researchers and volunteers worked together across borders to create them and save lives. Importance of COVID-19 vaccination should reach among adolescents to change their mind set from vaccine hesitancy to vaccine confidence. The present study is thus entitled as '***A Critical analysis of COVID-19 Vaccine Hesitancy among adolescents*** '

Definition of Key Terms

COVID-19

The name of the illness caused by the coronavirus SARS-CoV-2. COVID-19 stands for "Coronavirus disease 2019"

Vaccine Hesitancy

Vaccine Hesitancy is a delay in acceptance, or refusal of vaccine despite the availability of vaccine services.

Adolescent

Adolescents are people aged from puberty to maturity. They are in a transitional stage of physical and psychological development that generally occurs during the period from puberty to legal adulthood.

Objectives

1. To analyse the attitude of adolescents towards COVID-19 Vaccine.
2. To identify the factors that cause vaccine hesitancy among adolescents.

Hypotheses

1. The attitude of Adolescents towards the COVID-19 Vaccine is not satisfactory.
2. There exist significant factors that cause vaccine hesitancy among adolescents.

Methodology

Method

The investigator adopted the survey method for the study as it affords opportunities for

determining the predominant conditions and it is essentially a technique of quantitative description of the characteristics of the sample selected for the study. Since the present study aims to find out the factors that cause vaccine hesitancy among adolescents, a normative survey was found suitable to the study.

Population

The population of the study involves adolescent students of the age range 18-19.

Sample

The sample selected for the study involves 125 adolescent students who had not been vaccinated yet, studying in different Colleges of Thiruvananthapuram and Kollam districts in Kerala state.

The tool used for the study

A Questionnaire having 15 questions was used for collecting relevant information related to the attitude of adolescents towards the COVID-19 Vaccine. The questions were all Yes /No types.

The procedure adopted for the study

The present study is online-based, due to the existing context of the Covid 19 pandemic. The questionnaire was administered to the sample through a google form. The completed response forms were analysed by using suitable statistical techniques such as the computation of percentages.

Analysis and Interpretation

The details of the analysis of data are presented in Table .1

Table 1: Analysis of factors causing Vaccine Hesitancy among Adolescents

SI No	Questions	Response (%)	
		Yes	No
1	Do you think that COVID-19 is a big threat in which vaccination is the first remedy?	60	40
2	Do you trust the efficacy of COVID-19 vaccine?	46	54
3	Do you concern about the side effect of COVID-19 vaccine	62	38
4	Do you bother about the misconceptions spread through social media?	78	22
5	Do you think that the fast production of the vaccine compromised its safety?	62	38
6	Do you agree the recommendations made by health agencies and WHO in relation to the safety measures of COVID-19 vaccine?	71	29
7	Do you concern about the pain and discomfort associated with vaccination?	65	35
8	Do you think that vaccine cause any long-term injury to the body?	61	39
9	Do you think that vaccine cause any sudden and harmful injury to the body?	46	54
10	Are you satisfied with the Vaccination Programs of Government and Health organizations?	56	44
11	Are you in a wait and see attitude towards COVID-19 vaccine?	71	29
12	Does high cost of vaccine made you to evade it?	30	70
13	Does lesser vaccine availability forced you to hesitates it?	25	75
14	Do you care the conflicting views shared by your friends and Peers?	81	19
15	Do you think that the clinical trial data is insufficient to trust its efficacy?	55	45

Table 1: Analysis of factors causing Vaccine Hesitancy among Adolescents

From Table 1, it is clear that 60% of adolescents opined COVID-19 is a big threat in which vaccination is the first remedy but 54% of them are suspicious of the efficacy of the COVID-19 vaccine. 62% of the sample acknowledged that they were all concerned about the side effects of the COVID-19 vaccine. While considering the misconceptions spread through social media, the majority (78%) of the adolescents revealed that they were all weird by these thoughts, 62% of the sample reflected that the fast production of the vaccine compromised its safety. 71% of the sample agreed on the recommendations made by health agencies and WHO in relation to the safety measures of COVID-19 vaccine at the same time 29% disagreed it. The data also unveil that above half (65%) of the sample concerned about the pain and discomfort associated with vaccination. 61% opined that vaccines cause long-term injury to the body at the same time only 46% reported that vaccine causes sudden and harmful injury to the body.

Analysis of the data concerning to the Vaccination Programs of Government and Health organizations, 44 % of the adolescents were dissatisfied with it and 71% of the sample was in 'wait and see' attitude towards COVID-19 vaccine. Few adolescents (25%) opined that the lesser availability of vaccine was a reason for the delay of vaccine intake whereas 30 % reported that high cost of vaccine made them to evade it. 81% of the sample revealed that they were critically influenced by the conflicting views shared by their friends and Peers on COVID-19 vaccines. But 55% of adolescents were not satisfied with the clinical trial data as it is insufficient to trust the efficacy of COVID-19 vaccine.

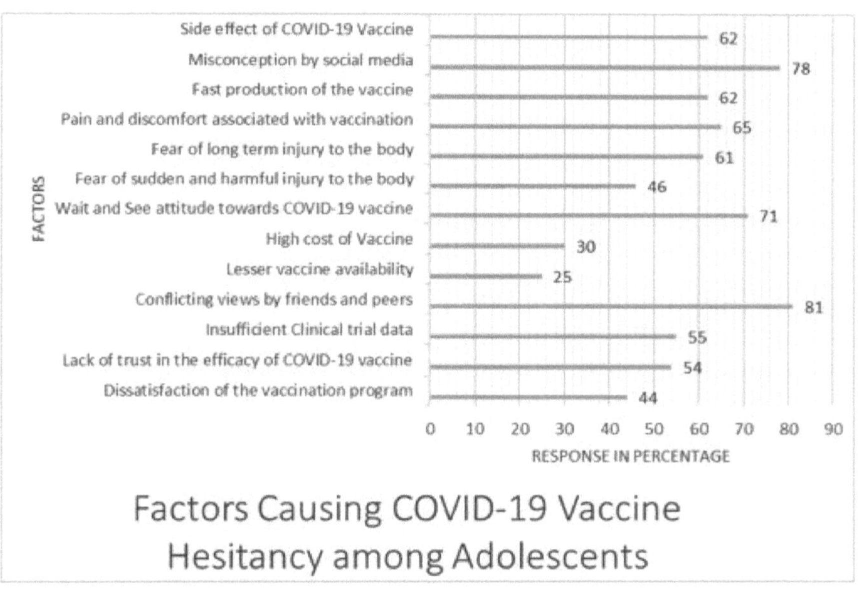

Figure1: Factors of COVID-19 Vaccine Hesitancy among Adolescents

Tenability of Hypotheses

Analysis of the data reveals that under the influence of peer pressure and social media, the majority of adolescents uphold a negative attitude towards the COVID-19 Vaccine. Hence, the proposed Hypothesis I, ***The attitude of Adolescents towards COVID-19 Vaccine is not satisfactory,*** is accepted. The findings also unveiled that most of the adolescents selected for the study were hesitant to take Covid 19 vaccine because of significant underlying factors, therefore Hypothesis II, ***There exist significant factors that cause vaccine hesitancy among adolescentsis*** also accepted.

Major findings

- Attitude of adolescents towards COVID-19 Vaccine was not satisfactory, 71% of adolescent were in 'wait and see' attitude.
- Vaccine Hesitancy among Adolescents were caused by significant factors such as concern about the side effect (62%), fast production of the vaccine (62%) and pain and discomfort associated with vaccination (65%).
- Majority (78%) of the sample bothered about the misconceptions of COVID- 19 vaccine spread through social media.
- Great majority of the adolescents (81%) revealed that the conflicting views shared by friends and Peers lead them to hesitate COVID-19 Vaccine.

Suggestions

Vaccines are effective interventions that can reduce the high burden of diseases globally. However, vaccine hesitancy, especially among adolescents is a pressing problem for public health. Vaccine education initiatives should be designed to reach among adolescents. Provision should be made to give accurate and timely information to answer the questions and concerns about vaccine. Systematic interventions are required from the part of public health authorities to reduce the levels of vaccines hesitancy among adolescents and to improve their acceptance. These interventions should take the form of revitalizing the trust in national health authorities and structured awareness campaigns that offer transparent information about the safety and efficacy of the vaccines and the technology that was utilized for its production.

Conclusion

The COVID-19 pandemic has led to a dramatic loss of human life worldwide and presents an unprecedented challenge to public health. To grow and develop in good health in this pandemic period of COVID-19, adolescents need information. Health services that are acceptable, equitable, appropriate and effective and safe and supportive environments provide opportunities to meaningfully participate in the interventions related to this pandemic. Since every COVID-19 infection gives the corona virus a chance to mutate, being vaccinated helps prevent variants and stop spreading of the disease. Only together people can overcome this pandemic. Hence the goal of the society should be to shift the mindset of adolescents from vaccine hesitancy to vaccine confidence.

Reference

Abdullahi, L. H., Kagina, B. M., Ndze, V. N., Hussey, G. D., & Wiysonge, C. S. (2020). Improving vaccination uptake among adolescents. The Cochrane database of systematic reviews, 1(1), CD011895. https://doi.org/10.1002/14651858.CD011895.pub2

Bagateli LE, Saeki EY, Fadda M, Agostoni C, Marchisio P, Milani GP(2021). COVID-19 Vaccine Hesitancy among Parents of Children and Adolescents Living in Brazil. Vaccines. 2021; 9(10):1115. https://doi.org/10.3390/vaccines9101115

Cadeddu, C., Castagna, C., Sapienza, M., Lanza, T. E., Messina, R., Chiavarini, M., Ricciardi, W., & de Waure, C. (2021). Understanding the determinants of vaccine hesitancy and vaccine confidence among adolescents: a systematic review. Human vaccines & immunotherapeutics, 1–17. Advance online publication. https://doi.org/10.1080/21645515.2021.1961466

Cadeddu, C., Sapienza, M., Castagna, C., Regazzi, L., Paladini, A., Ricciardi, W., & Rosano, A. (2021). Vaccine Hesitancy and Trust in the Scientific Community in Italy: Comparative Analysis from Two Recent Surveys. Vaccines, 9(10), 1206. https://doi.org/10.3390/vaccines9101206

Larson, H. J., Jarrett, C., Eckersberger, E., Smith, D. M., & Paterson, P. (2014). Understanding vaccine hesitancy around vaccines and vaccination from a global perspective: a systematic review of published literature, 2007-2012. Vaccine, 32(19), 2150–2159. https://doi.org/10.1016/j.vaccine.2014.01.081

Miko, D., Costache, C., Colosi, H. A., Neculicioiu, V., & Colosi, I. A. (2019). Qualitative Assessment of Vaccine Hesitancy in Romania. Medicina (Kaunas, Lithuania), 55(6), 282. https://doi.org/10.3390/medicina55060282

CHAPTER FOUR

Importance and Relevance of Vaccine

The importance of vaccination

Vaccines have caused some uncertainty and misunderstanding. Vaccinations, on the other hand, are a vital element of both personal and public health. Vaccines help to prevent the spread of diseases that are contagious, hazardous, and deadly. Measles, polio, mumps, chicken pox, whooping cough, diphtheria, and HPV are among them.

The smallpox vaccine was the first to be discovered. Smallpox was a fatal disease. In the last century, it killed between 300 million and 500 million people all across the world. The disease was eventually eradicated after people received the vaccine. It is the only illness that has been entirely eradicated. Others, such as polio, are now on the verge of reaching that position.

What are Vaccines?

A vaccine (also known as an immunization) is a method of increasing your body's natural immunity to a disease before you become ill. This prevents you from contracting the sickness and spreading it to others.

A weakened variant of the disease germ is delivered into your body for most vaccinations. This is normally accomplished by administering a shot to the leg or arm. Antibodies are produced by your body in response to invading microorganisms (antigens). Antibodies linger in your body for a long time after that. They often stay with you for the rest of your life. If you are ever exposed to the disease again, your body will fight it off and you will never get it.

Some infections, such as cold virus strains, are quite mild. However, some diseases, such as smallpox or polio, can have life-altering consequences. They have the potential to be fatal. As a result, it's critical to keep your body safe from these infections.

How does immunity work?

To resist invading pathogens that could make you sick or harm you, your body develops a defence mechanism. It's referred to as your immune system. Your body needs be exposed to various microorganisms in order to strengthen your immune system. When your body is initially exposed to a germ, it generates antibodies to help you fight it. However, this takes time, and you normally become ill before your antibodies have developed. Antibodies, on the other hand, remain in your body once you have them. As a result, the antibodies will target that germ the next time you're exposed to it, and you won't get sick.

Path to improve health

Vaccines are required for everyone. Infants, children, teenagers, and adults are all advised to use them. There are vaccine schedules that are commonly approved. They specify which immunizations are required and when they should be administered. The majority of immunizations are administered to youngsters. By the time they turn six, kids should have received 14 different immunizations. Some of these are presented as a series of images. Some vaccines are combined to reduce the number of doses required.

Immunization, according to the American Academy of Family Physicians (AAFP), is critical in avoiding the spread of dangerous diseases. Vaccines are especially crucial for at-risk groups including young children and the elderly. The AAFP provides vaccination advice, immunization regimens, and disease-specific vaccine information.

Side effects of vaccines

After you or your kid receives a vaccine, there may be adverse effects. They're usually not too bad. Redness or swelling at the injection site are two of them. A low-grade fever can occur in children. These signs and symptoms normally disappear after a day or two. There have been reports of more significant side effects, but these are uncommon.

Before a vaccine is approved as safe and effective, it goes through years of development and testing. Before authorizing a vaccination, scientists and doctors at the US Food and Drug Administration (FDA) examine the research. They also inspect the facilities where the vaccinations are made to ensure that all regulations are followed. The FDA continues to monitor the vaccine's use when it is made available to the general population. It ensures that there are no safety concerns. Vaccines are completely safe. The advantages of using them far outweigh any potential side effects.

Things to consider:

Vaccines have been the subject of many misconceptions. On the internet, there are many fallacies and false comments about vaccines. Here are the answers to five of the most common vaccine questions and misconceptions.

- **Vaccines don't cause autism**

There has been no evidence of a link between vaccines and the risk of developing autism in research. The sole paper that claimed there was a correlation has been debunked. Its author, a doctor, lost his medical license. According to research, infants may be born with autism before receiving any immunizations.

- **Vaccines are not overly taxing on an infant's immune system**

The immune systems of infants are capable of handling far more than what immunizations provide. Every day, they are exposed to hundreds of bacteria and viruses. Adding a few more with a vaccine does not increase the amount of damage their immune systems can take.

- **Vaccines do not contain any poisons that are harmful to your health**

Some vaccines contain trace levels of chemicals that, in big doses, could be dangerous. Formaldehyde, aluminum, and mercury are among them. The amount used in vaccines, however, is so little that they are totally safe. For example, by the age of two, a child will have ingested 4mg of aluminum from all immunizations. In 6 months, a breastfed baby will consume 10mg. In 6 months, a soy-based formula delivers 120mg. Furthermore, newborns have 10 times the amount of formaldehyde in their bodies that is present in a vaccine. Vaccines have never contained the dangerous form of mercury.

- **Vaccines do not cause the diseases that they are supposed to protect you from**

This is a prevalent misunderstanding, especially when it comes to the flu vaccine. Many individuals believe that taking a flu vaccine makes them sick. Flu injections, on the other hand, contain dead viruses, so you can't become sick from them. You may get modest symptoms comparable to the sickness even if the vaccine utilizes attenuated live viruses. However, you do not have the disease.

- **Vaccines are still required in the United States, despite low illness rates**

Because of our high immunization rate, several diseases are uncommon in the United States. However, they have not been eradicated from other parts of the globe. Anyone who isn't vaccinated is at risk of contracting a disease brought to the United States by a foreign traveler. Vaccination is the only way to keep infection rates low.

Why is the COVID-19 vaccine both safe and necessary?

Now that effective COVID-19 vaccinations have been produced and are being delivered to the general public, it is critical for people to understand the benefits of the vaccines and why they much outweigh any minor potential side effects or inconvenience.

According to Michael Saag, M.D., professor of medicine at the University of Alabama at Birmingham Division of Infectious Diseases, the possibility of serious complications for anyone who contracts the virus, as well as the public health consequences of the pandemic continuing, are compelling reasons to get vaccinated. But what else should the general people be aware of?

The COVID-19 vaccine can assist you from contracting the virus

COVID-19 vaccinations have been licensed after being tested in clinical trials and demonstrating that the vaccine considerably reduces the risk of catching the virus.

Even if you receive the virus, the COVID-19 vaccination may help you avoid becoming extremely ill, based on what has been proven regarding vaccines for other diseases. Getting vaccinated may help protect individuals around you, especially those who are at higher risk of severe COVID-19 sickness.

The full worth of the vaccine, according to Saag, may be recognized when we examine what would happen if the vaccine development had failed.

He compares the speedy discovery of a safe, highly successful vaccination to a "home run" as well as an occurrence that could be considered divine intervention.

The COVID-19 vaccine is a vital instrument in the fight against the pandemic

Stopping a pandemic necessitates the use of all available tools. Wearing masks and keeping a safe distance from people can help minimize your risk of contracting the virus or spreading it to others, but these precautions are insufficient. Vaccines work with your immune system to ensure that if you are exposed to the virus, you will be prepared to fight it.

The best protection against COVID-19 is a combination of getting vaccinated and following CDC advice to protect yourself and others. Ending the COVID-19 pandemic will put an end to the virus's expanding detrimental impact on education, the economy, health care, and countless other aspects of society.

Vaccines have no effect on or interaction with our DNA

COVID-19 vaccines are mRNA (messenger RNA) vaccines, which are a new type of vaccine. These mRNA vaccines instruct our cells to produce a non-lethal fragment of protein known as the spike protein. The spike protein is present on the virus's surface. COVID-19 mRNA never reaches the cell nucleus, which is where DNA (genetic material) is kept. Once within your muscle cells, the instructions are used to produce the protein piece, and then the instructions are broken down and discarded.

The cell then deposits the protein fragment on its surface. When the immune system detects the protein, it begins to mount an immunological response and produce antibodies in order to combat the infection. Our bodies have learned how to protect themselves from infection towards the end of this procedure.

COVID-19 immunization is a less risky technique to aid in the development of protection

COVID-19 can cause major, life-threatening consequences, as evidenced by the hundreds of patients who require hospitalization every day at UAB. Even though certain groups are affected less severely than others due to age, health, and other variables, no one can predict how COVID-19 will impact an individual.

COVID-19 may provide some natural protection in the form of immunity. However, doctors are unsure how long that immunity lasts, and the risk of serious disease and death from COVID-19 far surpasses any natural immunity benefits. Getting vaccinated causes an antibody response, which protects you from contracting the disease without having to go through it. Experts are looking into both natural immunity and vaccine-induced immunity as essential aspects of COVID-19. Officials from the health-care system intend to keep the public updated on new developments.

As a doctor and a COVID-19 survivor, Saag believes that getting infected with the virus is the least desirable and risky way to gain immunity.

"It was a nightmare." "For eight days, I was terrified of what the next day would bring," Saag remarked. "I'd keep an eye on my oxygen level. If I had to be hospitalized and receive intensive care, I knew what I was in for. Every day, I would wake up feeling better, convinced that I had overcome the problem, only to have the symptoms flare up again in the evening. For eight nights, it felt like a scene from 'Groundhog Day.' The vaccine can prevent such an encounter, which, as we all know, not everyone survives. As a result, getting the vaccine is a no-brainer."

Conclusion

Because of the pandemic's sensitivity to time, recent research has mostly focused on COVID-19 as a central topic in epidemiology. Much of the available research has concentrated on the development of vaccinations, the availability of testing, and technical instructions for the public to follow in order to take precautions such as social distancing and wearing face masks (Burki, 2020; Worby and Colin J., 2020; Meredith, 2020; Chughtai et al., 2020). Our initiative analyses how the COVID-19 pandemic is influencing the entire world, from economic ramifications to changes in how people live, work, and socialize, in order to improve our existing understanding of the pandemic.

We hope that our project can provide deeper insight into how COVID-19 is affecting the world and our daily lives through two case studies in Shanghai and New York State, in terms of their distinct governmental and public responses to the epidemic.

"The name Digital Humanities thus describes not just a collective singular but also the humanities in the plural, capable of addressing and engaging different subject areas across media, language, place, and history," writes Anne Burdick. However, despite its diversity, the Digital Humanities are united by a focus on creating, connecting, interpreting, and cooperating."

By combining Mandarin-outlet popular and scholarly sources in our comparative analysis, we seek to bring hitherto segregated scholarships in China and the United States together to investigate the effectiveness of preventative measures. Both regions contracted a large number of cases, but the outcomes were different, with Shanghai reporting few new cases from local transmission and New York seeing a second surge.

We discovered that the policies and methods underpinning Shanghai's effectiveness in reducing COVID-19 were dependent on people's compliance and participation by comparing Shanghai and New York. The use of facemasks, traveler testing, and rigorous lockdown regulations in highly afflicted areas (including delivery-only grocery alternatives) are among the most successful approaches in decreasing the number of COVID-19 cases and deaths, according to our analysis of our data set.

References: -

- https://familydoctor.org/the-importance-of-vaccinations/
- https://www.uab.edu/news/youcanuse/item/11797-why-it-s-safe-and/
- https://datamovers.humspace.ucla.edu/conclusion/

CHAPTER FIVE

India's Vaccine History: The March Of The Vaccines

Introduction

The Indian economy is one of the world's fastest-expanding economies. The obstacles of getting life-saving vaccines to the intended recipients must be addressed using existing knowledge and lessons learned in the past. There are various crucial factors to consider when deciding whether or not a vaccine is ideal. Vaccines save lives, enhance health, especially in children, improve quality of life, and minimize antibiotic resistance very efficiently. Vaccines are currently available for 26 infectious illnesses, with many more in development. India has a lengthy history of vaccine production, with the World Health Organization (WHO) recognizing the Haffkine Institute as a prequalified vaccine producer before the country gained independence from Britain in 1947.

VACCINATION

Source: www.ruralhealthinfo.org

Early in the twentieth century, obstacles arose in the spread of smallpox vaccination, typhoid vaccine trials among Indian army soldiers, and the establishment of vaccine centers in nearly all of India's states. Despite the fact that disease prevention was implemented in India, the country's vaccination history has been marked by reluctance, rejection, and a tardy adoption of vaccination. Vaccination is a proven and cost-effective measure for child survival1. Every country in the world has an immunisation programme to administer certain vaccines to specific recipients, with a special focus on pregnant women, infants, and toddlers, who are at a higher risk of diseases that can be prevented with vaccines. In 1798, the first vaccination (for smallpox) was discovered. The eradication of smallpox sickness from the earth has been the most notable result of these endeavors. Vaccines and vaccination have a long history, dating back to the first attempt to prevent disease in society. There are limited descriptions of disease occurrence from India; nonetheless, one of the finest documented smallpox outbreaks occurred in Goa in 1545 AD, when an estimated 8,000 children died. Smallpox is occasionally referred to as the 'Indian Plague' by historians and physicians, implying that the disease was once widespread in India. In India, inoculation was common. It was defined as "the process of injecting an infective agent into a healthy person, which causes often mild disease and protects that individual from future serious disease." In India, vaccination was widely used.

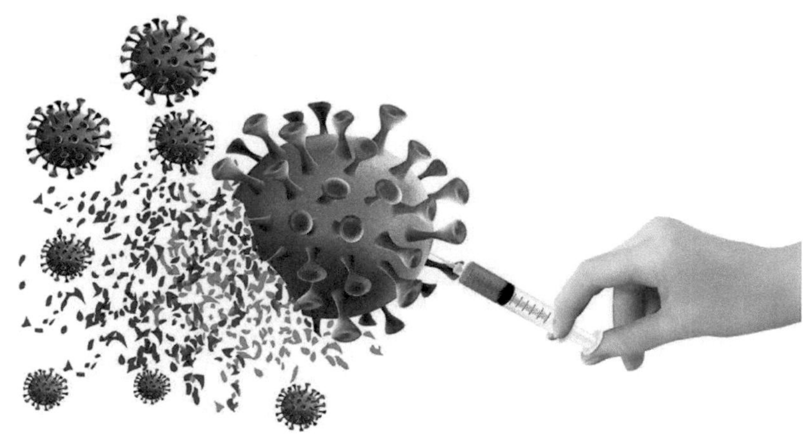

Source: www.chamber.org

Vaccination in India

In May 1802 the first doses of smallpox vaccine lymph arrived in India. On June 14, 18026, Anna Dusthall, a three-year-old girl from Bombay (now Mumbai), became the first person in India to get a smallpox vaccine. Officials from the Indian Medical Services made special efforts to popularise smallpox immunisation. The general public's uptake was poor for a variety of reasons, including the necessity to pay a little charge for vaccination, belief in the process of inoculation and that the disease was divine wrath, and many other fallacies. Some Hindus objected to the vaccine since it came from a cow, which is considered a sacred animal. The Bombay vaccination system, which began in 1827, was heavily relied on touring/traveling vaccinators who were in charge of vaccination circles or subdivisions. Later on, the Bombay technique became the most generally used method in other Indian provinces. In 1892, India implemented the Compulsory Vaccination Act in order to increase smallpox vaccination coverage and lessen the pandemic. In 1962, India launched the National

Smallpox Eradication Program (NSEP), with the goal of vaccinating the whole population within three years. In the 'attack phase,' the goal was to reach 80% coverage, while in the maintenance phase,' all newborns, babies, and children aged 5, 10, and 15 were to be vaccinated. However, coverage remained low after five years of implementation, and outbreaks continued to be reported. India has a large number of HIV-positive and AIDS-affected people. To stop the epidemic, a safe, effective, and widely available preventive AIDS vaccine, together with other preventive treatments, is urgently needed.

Introduction of new Vaccines

The understanding of the decision-making process in the introduction of new vaccines helps establish why vaccines are adopted or not. It also contributes to building a sustainable demand for vaccines in a country. The findings revealed that the actors from different sectors at the policy level were involved in the decision-making process in the introduction of new vaccines. They included policy-makers from the ministries of health and family welfare, finance, and local government and rural development; academicians; researchers; representatives from professional associations; development partners; and members of different committees on EPI. They contributed to the introduction of new vaccines in their own capacity. India approved different vaccines under emergency use authorization but the distribution of vaccines and vaccination of a huge population was a challenging task.

Vaccination efforts continued with varying degrees of success until 1939 when World War II broke out. Vaccination programmes, while still a priority for local government, became a war victim. Vaccination coverage declined, and India reported the highest number of smallpox cases in the previous two decades in 1944-1945. When World War II ended, the focus was redirected to smallpox vaccination, and cases dropped dramatically. The typhoid vaccine trials in India between 1904 and 1908 were another significant event during this time.

Tuberculosis was thought to be a leading cause of death and morbidity. In May 1948, the Indian government issued a press release declaring that tuberculosis had reached "epidemic proportions" in the country and that, "after careful thought," it had decided to administer BCG vaccination on a restricted scale and under rigorous supervision as a control mechanism. BCG research began in India in 1948 as a pilot effort in two locations. In practically all of India's states, the BCG vaccination was made mandatory in schools in 1949.

Following India's declaration of smallpox-free status in 1977, the country opted to initiate the Expanded Programme of Immunization (EPI) in 1978, which included the introduction of BCG, OPV, DPT, and typhoid-paratyphoid vaccines. When the immunisation was included in the Prime Minister's 20-point plan, it gained even more importance.

COVID -19

Despite the fact that human history is littered with large-scale tragedies, COVID-19 stands out in several respects. It was not unusual due to the fact that it was highly contagious. That's something we've seen before. The media and worldwide lockdown are two distinct characteristics of this calamity. We had no idea what this disease was at first, but we knew it was killing people. We watched as healthcare providers in nations such as Italy and Spain were forced to make life-or-death decisions. We were cut off from all of our usual sources of comfort and connection, and we sat alone in our houses, watching the horror unfold in real-time. There was a distinct sense of dread in the air.

"Health is wealth," as they say. The saving is much more important during a pandemic, such as COVID-19, when the impact of health infrastructure may be seen in nearly every aspect of life. Every country strives to improve the quality of health care it provides to its residents. The coronavirus disease (COVID-19) pandemic and its response have created unique issues in the medical area, as well as in the scientific, political, economic, and ethical realms.

Since the founding of Biological E Ltd., India's first privately-funded vaccination company, in 1953, additional companies have begun to push public-private collaborations. Recently, India's Prime Minister pushed scientists to develop a COVID-19 vaccine. Vaccine research studies have been carried out by the Serum Institute of India, Bharat Biotech, Premas Biotech, and Zydus Cadila. For a long time, India's Serum Institute has developed tetanus, influenza, rabies, measles, and mumps immunizations. It is now collaborating with Codagenix on a vaccine, including a live-attenuated COVID-19 vaccine. The vaccine will be produced at a low cost, according to the Serum Institute. It has begun animal trials in partnership with the University of Wisconsin and FluGen Inc., and with the support of Thomas Jefferson University, it hopes to develop a novel one-drop nasal vaccine against COVID-19 called "CoroFlu." Zydus Cadila, a company based in Gujarat, India, has developed ZyCoV-D, a COVID-19 vaccine that is currently in phase II clinical trials. Diphtheria, Tetanus, Pertussis (DTP), Influenza (type B), Measles, Mumps, Rubella (MMR), Typhoid, and other diseases have all been vaccinated with it in the past.

Origin and Transmission

The coronavirus disease 19 (COVID-19) is a highly contagious and dangerous viral infection caused by the severe acute respiratory syndrome coronavirus 2 (SARS-CoV-2) virus, which first appeared in Wuhan, China, and has since spread throughout the world. Bats could be the primary reservoir, according to genomic analysis. SARS-CoV-2 is phylogenetically related to severe acute respiratory syndrome-like (SARS-like) bat viruses. It spread from person to person via droplets and touch, but there should be no uncertainty about airborne, fecal, or intrauterine transmission. In clinical studies, only a few broad-spectrum antiviral medicines have been tested against COVID-19, with clinical recovery.

On the 30th of January 2020, it was labeled a pandemic and a health emergency of international concern. In reaction to the global outbreak, harsh global containment and quarantine measures were implemented around the world. COVID-19 is a new threat to dental professionals and patients, as there is a high chance of cross-infection between them.

Despite being identified in the 1960s, human coronavirus still requires substantial research to fully comprehend. Coronaviruses have created pandemics since the new millennium began. The initial coronavirus outbreaks, SARS-CoV and MERS-CoV, caused socioeconomic and psychological harm in the past. The novel coronavirus outbreak (COVID-19) will benefit from our previous experience in dealing with similar disasters.

This unprecedented community health problem is terrifying the world, causing clinical, psychological, and emotional distress, as well as health system breakdown and economic slowness in approximately 200 countries. COVID-19 is a highly virulent and pathogenic COVID-19 viral infection that is transmitted by inhaling infected droplets or coming into contact with infected droplets. It belongs to the genus Coronavirus, which has a high mutation rate in the Coronaviridae family. Asymptomatic pyrexia, dry cough, sore throat, breathlessness, tiredness, body aches, fatigue, myalgia, nausea, vomiting, and diarrhea to severe consolidation and pneumonia, acute respiratory distress syndrome (ARDS), and multiple organ dysfunction leading to death with a case fatality rate of 2 to 3%.

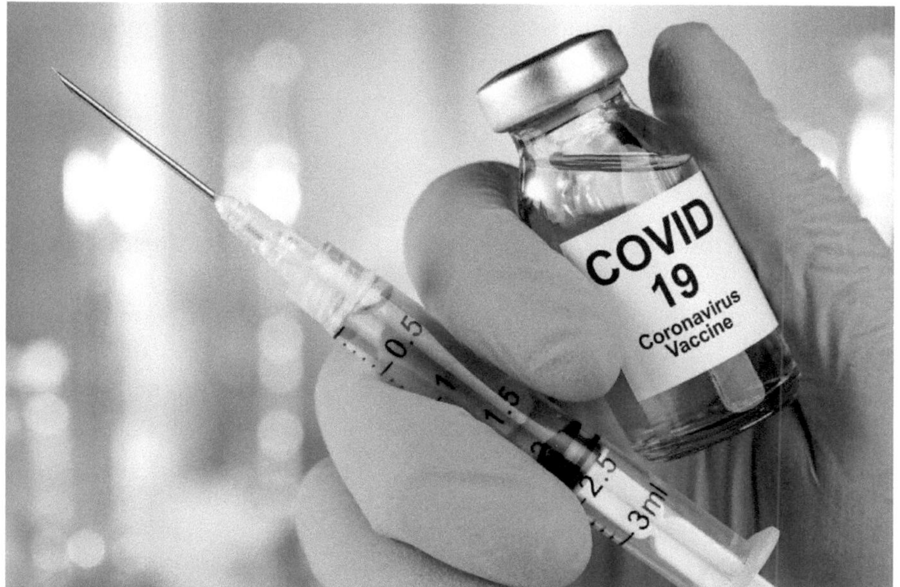

Source: www.news18.com

The elderly and those with co-existing morbidities such as diabetes, hypertension, and malignancies accounted for the bulk of COVID-19 mortality. It would ensure that the greatest number of lives could be spared, therefore reinforcing this critical ethical concept. It also satisfies the goal of minimizing mortality and illness burden from the COVID-19 pandemic, as stated in the WHO SAGE values framework's principle of human well-being. Furthermore, the vaccinations have yet to be demonstrated effective against COVID-19 infection that is asymptomatic.

Social Distancing

Isolation and quarantine (more severe kinds of social isolation) have been linked to sadness and anxiety. We can expect to observe similar impacts when incarcerated persons become estranged from their loved ones, robbed of personal liberties, and without a sense of purpose as their routine and livelihood are disrupted. 5 This might lead to feelings of frustration, boredom, low mood, and even depression. Fear of contagion and a lack of clarity surrounding social distancing standards may cause anxiety, which is sometimes exacerbated by less trustworthy media sources that heighten confusion and fearmongering.

Daily routines that include a healthy lifestyle, hobbies, virtual social connections, and mindfulness are suggested for the general population. Social distancing has been identified by the World Health Organization and the Centers for Disease Control as the most efficient strategy to reduce distances of 2 meters or 6 feet between people. Any gathering of more than ten individuals should be avoided or performed virtually in general.

Conclusion

India benefited from early achievements in vaccine research and development, as well as public-sector domestic production, but it is increasingly unable to supply the growing demand for UIP vaccines. The availability of UIP vaccinations from the commercial sector is declining in India and around the world. As a result, India (and every other country) must establish their own national vaccine policy while remaining within its budgetary constraints.

India has already sold difficult vaccines such as the pentavalent rotavirus vaccine. India is unique in that it has gained expertise in vaccine production at a low per-unit cost. Thanks to the low-cost vaccination that made history, new items against COVID-19 will be of major service in many low-income countries throughout the world, benefiting millions of individuals who cannot afford pricy vaccines. Although the government provides vaccination services to the majority of the people in India, the private sector should not be overlooked because it has the potential to boost total vaccine coverage. The government may train and reward a broader range of private-sector health experts to assist in the delivery of vaccines, particularly in low-income states with the highest birth cohorts. We know that social distance is the most effective measure at the moment, based on China's experience with new coronavirus pneumonia. By practicing physical distancing, you can be a hero and break the COVID-19 transmission cycle.

References

Lahariya, C. (2014). A brief history of vaccines & vaccination in India. The Indian journal of medical research, 139(4), 491.

Madhavi, Y. (2005). Vaccine policy in India. PLoS medicine, 2(5), e127.

Sur, D. (2016). Challenges in new vaccine introduction in a national program in India. Indian journal of public health, 60(3), 171.

Chakraborty, C., & Agoramoorthy, G. (2020). India's cost-effective COVID-19 vaccine development initiatives. Vaccine, 38(50), 7883.

Gupta, S. S., Nair, G. B., Arora, N. K., & Ganguly, N. K. (2013). Vaccine development and deployment: opportunities and challenges in India.

Vaccine, 31, B43-B53.

Excler, J. L., Kochhar, S., Kapoor, S., Das, S., Bahri, J., Ghosh, M. D., ... & Chataway, M. (2008). Preparedness for AIDS vaccine trials in India. Indian Journal of Medical Research, 127(6), 531.

Verma, A., Rana, A., Monga, H., Chaudhary, A., & Singh, J. (2021, September). Distribution Management of Drugs/medicines and vaccines vis-à-vis Free Drugs Service Initiative (FDSI) of Ministry of Health and Family Welfare (MoHFW), Government of India in the Indian States. In 2021 9th International Conference on Reliability, Infocom Technologies and Optimization (Trends and Future Directions)(ICRITO) (pp. 1-5). IEEE.

Shereen, M. A., Khan, S., Kazmi, A., Bashir, N., & Siddique, R. (2020). COVID-19 infection: Origin, transmission, and characteristics of human coronaviruses. Journal of advanced research, 24, 91.

Madabhavi, I., Sarkar, M., & Kadakol, N. (2020). COVID-19: a review. Monaldi Archives for Chest Disease, 90(2).

Misra, V., Bhardwaj, A., Bhardwaj, S., & Misra, S. (2020). Novel COVID-19–Origin, emerging challenges, recent trends, transmission routes and Control-A review. Journal of Contemporary Orthodontics, 58(4), 1.

Kahn, J. S., & McIntosh, K. (2005). History and recent advances in coronavirus discovery. The Pediatric infectious disease journal, 24(11), S223-S227.

Jahangir, M. A., Muheem, A., & Rizvi, M. F. (2020). Coronavirus (COVID-19): history, current knowledge and pipeline medications. Int J Pharm Pharmacol 2020; 4: 140. Doi: 10.31531/2581, 3080(2).

Venkatesh, A., & Edirappuli, S. (2020). Social distancing in covid-19: what are the mental health implications?. Bmj, 369.

CHAPTER SIX

Vaccine Schedule of India

Introduction

On January 16, 2021, India began administering COVID-19 vaccinations. India had provided approximately 1.18 billion doses in total as of November 23, 2021, including the first and second doses of currently licensed vaccines. In India, 80% of the eligible population received at least one vaccination, and the number of fully vaccinated people has overtaken the number of partially vaccinated people.

Oxford vaccine (called Covishield) and Covaxin (made locally by Bharat Biotech) were the first to be licensed in India, and since then, many more have joined the line, including Sputnik, Jonson&Jhonson, and Moderna vaccines.

The vaccination campaign was launched by the Indian government in three stages.

Priority allocation stages for vaccine roll-out

Stage 1
3% of population

Health care workers

Social care workers

Stage 2
20% of population

Over 65s and high risk

Stage 3
20% + of population

Further priority groups

Note: No country will receive vaccines for more than 20% of their population before others in Covax financing group

Source: WHO BBC

Source:bbc.com

First Phase

The vaccination effort, in which beneficiaries would have no option between the two vaccines available in India — Covishield, and Covaxin — has been organised in stages, with priority groups including healthcare, social care professionals, severely vulnerable groups, and frontline workers identified.

During this first phase, healthcare employees from both the public and private sectors, including Integrated Child Development Services (ICDS) staff, will receive the vaccine. In the first wave of vaccination, three crore health care and frontline personnel would receive free COVID vaccination. In the first phase, almost 300 million people were vaccinated, and in the second phase, nearly 600 million people were vaccinated.

Each vaccination facility will offer either Covaxin or Covishield, not both. Vaccine rollouts were slow in the beginning because people were apprehensive of the vaccine due to safety reasons and misinformation.

On Friday, the Ministry reviewed the functioning of Cowin, the online digital platform built by the Ministry to be used to drive the vaccination programme. Adequate doses of both vaccinations have already been supplied across the country to all States/UTs.

The platform will allow for real-time monitoring of vaccine stockpiles, storage temperature, and individualised tracking of COVID-19 vaccination recipients. It goes on to say that the platform allows national and state managers to see and categorise beneficiary data by gender, age, and co-morbidity.

Challenges

One of the most difficult challenges in immunisation is the insufficient distribution of cold chains across India's many states. Out of India's 29 000 cold chain points, 52 percent are concentrated in just six states, accounting for a third of the population: Maharashtra, Karnataka, Tamil Nadu, Rajasthan, Gujarat, and Andhra Pradesh.

While there is a requirement for adequate cold storage facilities, India's vaccine wastage has increased due to a lack of the required number of beneficiaries per session, a shortage of qualified vaccinators, and limited shelf life of the vaccine after vial opening.

Individual Indian citizens have to register on the Cowin or Arogya Setu portal earlier this year in order to acquire a COVID-19 immunisation. Because of the limited number of vaccine slots, fewer administrations occurred during the first five months of the vaccination programme (phases 1–4). However, a lack of proper internet access in remote regions would be a significant hurdle to the vaccination push. Individual Indian citizens have to register on the Cowin or Arogya Setu portal earlier this year in order to acquire a COVID-19 vaccination. Because of the limited number of vaccine slots, fewer administrations occurred during the first five months of the vaccination programme (phases 1–4). However, a lack of proper internet access in remote regions would be a significant challenge to the vaccination push.

Second Phase

All inhabitants above the age of 60, residents between the ages of 45 and 60 with one or more qualifying comorbidities, and any health care or frontline worker who did not receive a dose during phase 1 were included in the next phase of the vaccination deployment. Anyone can schedule an appointment using the co-Win website or the Arogya setu app.

Starting at 9 a.m., the latest edition of the Co-Win application, which is at the heart of India's immunisation programme, will be available for registration. Citizens will be able to register for the vaccine and schedule an appointment through the Co-Win 2.0 site or other IT apps such as Arogya Setu, etc., at any time and from anywhere.

Vaccines will be accessible at private hospitals in the second phase of the vaccination campaign. While it will be provided free of charge in government hospitals, private institutions are authorised to charge no more than $250 per person every dose—150 for vaccines and 100 for administrative costs.

For each dose, a beneficiary will only have one live appointment at any one moment. Appointments for any day at a Covid Vaccination Centre (CVC) will be closed at 3:00 p.m. on the day for which the slots were opened, according to the statement. On the 29th day following the date of the first dose appointment, a slot for the second dose will be reserved at the same CVC. If a beneficiary cancels a first dosage appointment, both dose appointments will be canceled. Those who are eligible can register at the Co-Win 2.0 portal using their cell phone number. A single mobile number can be used to register up to four beneficiaries. However, save for the mobile number, all people registered on a single mobile number will have nothing in common. Each such beneficiary's Photo ID Card Number must be unique. People can use whatever they choose.

Each such beneficiary must have a unique Photo ID Card Number. People can use any of the seven identity documents to register for online services. Aadhar Card/Letter, Electoral Photo Identity Card (EPIC), passport, driving license, PAN Card, NPR Smart Card, and pension document with a photograph are among the documents required.

Eligibility was expanded to all inhabitants over the age of 45 on April 1st. On April 8, Prime Minister Narendra Modi announced a four-day Teeka Utsav ("Vaccine Festival") from April 11 to 14, with the purpose of speeding up the programme by vaccinating as many eligible residents as possible. By the end of the Utsav, India had administered over 111 million vaccine doses.

Challenges

After cold storage and other logistical difficulties, the spread of misinformation, particularly in India, is one of the most significant challenges for the COVID-19 immunisation programme. Globally, there has been an increase in disinformation during the COVID-19 epidemic, forcing WHO to host the first infodemiology conference. 11 The COVID-19 pandemic has resulted in more widespread misinformation than any other pandemic or epidemic in history, owing to the increase of content available on multimedia platforms. 12 and 13 Following the first reported case in India in January, key communication channels were inundated with an infodemic of fake news on every aspect of the pandemic, from its origin to its cure.

Misleading information about a single religion is especially common in India, where Hinduism is practised by the majority of the population (more than 80% of the overall population), followed by Islam (more than 13 percent of the total population). 15 members of the Hindu community were exposed to bogus news suggesting that cow meat was utilised in vaccine manufacture. Similarly, members of the Muslim community were subjected to bogus news alleging traces of pork in the vaccine.

Third Phase

The DCGI licenced Russia's Sputnik V vaccine for emergency use in India on April 12. In September 2020, the country conducted a phase 3 trial, which revealed 91.6 percent efficacy. [44] Dr. Reddy's Laboratories, the local distributor, claimed that the vaccine would be available in India by late May 2021.

On May 1, India will start the third phase of its coronavirus vaccination campaign, in which all people above the age of 18 will be eligible to be vaccinated.

The government states unequivocally, "Only self-registration and advance appointments for those between the ages of 18 and 45." There will be no walk-ins."

While the second dosage of Covaxin must be administered between 28 and 42 days after the first dose, the second dose of Covishield must be administered between 28 and 56 days after the first dose. COVID-19 vaccines, like many other vaccinations, have the potential to cause side effects. The most common side effects, according to India's Union Ministry of Health and Family Welfare, include discomfort or swelling at the injection site, fever, irritability, and headaches.

Fourth Phase

From January 3, 2022, India will begin distributing Covid-19 vaccines to children aged 15 to 18.

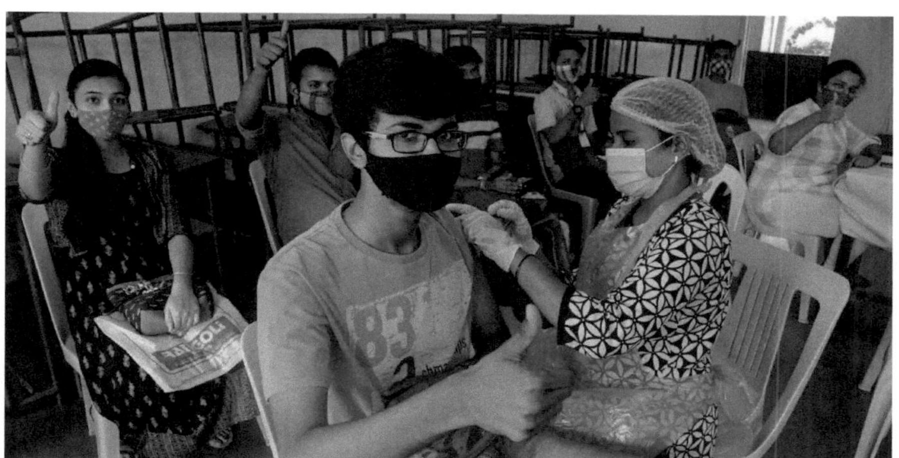

Source:onmanorama.com

The Union Health Ministry has announced that Bharat Biotech's Covaxin will be the only vaccination delivered to eligible recipients aged 15 to 18. The vaccination will be available to children born in 2007 and earlier.

How to register for vaccination

- Beneficiaries can self-register online through an existing account on Co-WIN. So, children can use their parents' existing CO-WIN accounts to book their slots
- Beneficiaries can also be registered onsite by the verifier/vaccinator
- They can also register by creating a new account through a unique mobile number
- They can also walk in to get their shots.

Charges

- Only COVAXIN will be given to children in the age group of 15-18 years
- All beneficiaries irrespective of their income status are entitled to get free shots at
- government vaccination centres
- However, those who opt for private hospitals or vaccination centres will have to pay the requisite fees.

In response to an increase in infections, India has begun offering priority groups booster doses of the Covid-19 vaccine.

Health and frontline professionals, as well as persons over 60 with comorbidities, are currently eligible to receive the vaccine.

The booster dose, or 'precautionary' dose as the government refers to it, is permitted beginning January 10. Boosters should be administered nine months following the second dose.

Some common side effects of covid-vaccine

On the arm where you got the shot:

- Pain
- Redness
- Swelling

Throughout the rest of your body:

- Tiredness
- Headache
- Muscle pain
- Chills
- Fever
- Nausea

Conclusion

In the past, India has successfully eradicated smallpox and polio. 2 Such precise planning and management can assist India in carrying out the ambitious COVID-19 vaccine effort. Authorities should invest in extensive vaccination planning, including work allocation and requirements assessment, all the way down to the lowest governance level.

India is in a unique position to produce low-cost medical, surgical, and vital generic medications for the rest of the globe. It is also common knowledge that India is the world's largest manufacturer and distributor of vaccines. The present COVID-19 epidemic has prompted quick development, emergency use authorisation, and unprecedented collaboration among stakeholders. Although vaccination may be a cost-effective method for people's survival and a higher quality of life, as well as for the resurgence of India's economy.

References

- World's largest vaccination drive in India: Challenges and recommendations 18 August 2021
- By Gladson Vaghela,Kapil Narain, Mashkur Abdulhamid Isa, Vaishnavi Kanisetti, Attaullah Ahmadi,Don Eliseo Lucero-Prisno III
- India's COVID-19 vaccination drive: key challenges and resolutions
- November 2021 By Priyanka Choudhary Indraj Singh
- Strategy for COVID-19 vaccination in India: the country with the second highest population and number of cases April,2021
- By Velayudhan Mohan Kumar, Seithikurippu R. Pandi-Perumal, Ilya Trakht & Sadras Panchatcharam Thyagarajan
- COVID-19: 80% of eligible population of India now inoculated; number of fully jabbed crosses partially vaccinated November 2021

By FPJ webdesk

- Coronavirus | Registration for next phase of vaccination on Co-WIN 2.0 portal to open on March 1 February,2021

By Hindu

- Coronavirus | 'Tika Utsav' is start of second big war against virus: Modi April,2021
- India begins third phase of vaccination drive by including all above 45
- Possible Side Effects After Getting a COVID-19 Vaccine January 2021

By NCIRD

CHAPTER SEVEN

India's COVID-19 vaccine deployment strategies

Introduction

On January 16, 2021, India began administering COVID-19 vaccines. As of January 4, 2022, India had administered over 1.53 billion doses in total, including the first and second doses of currently approved vaccines. In India, 88 percent of the eligible population has received at least one vaccination, and 63 percent is fully vaccinated.

The Oxford–AstraZeneca vaccine (manufactured under license by Serum Institute of India under the trade name Covishield) and Covaxin were initially approved in India (a vaccine developed locally by Bharat Biotech). They have since been joined by the Sputnik V (manufactured under license by Dr. Reddy's Laboratories, with additional production beginning in September from Serum Institute of India), Moderna vaccines, Johnson & Johnson vaccine, and ZyCoV-D (a vaccine developed locally by Zydus Cadil and other vaccine candidates undergoing local clinical trials).

The first case of new coronavirus infections was discovered a year ago in China's Wuhan province. Efforts were focused on avoiding and reducing transmission during the early stages of the disease. COVID-19 vaccinations that are effective are urgently needed, according to a global review of herd immunity. Coronavirus disease 2019 (COVID-19) is the most serious public health threat of the twenty-first century, affecting millions of individuals around the world. Due to the lack of a broad and effective treatment for COVID-19 or a prevention strategy for SARS-CoV-2 dissemination, the outbreak of severe acute respiratory syndrome coronavirus 2 (SARS-CoV-2) has sparked an unprecedented effort from the scientific community in the development of new vaccines on various platforms.

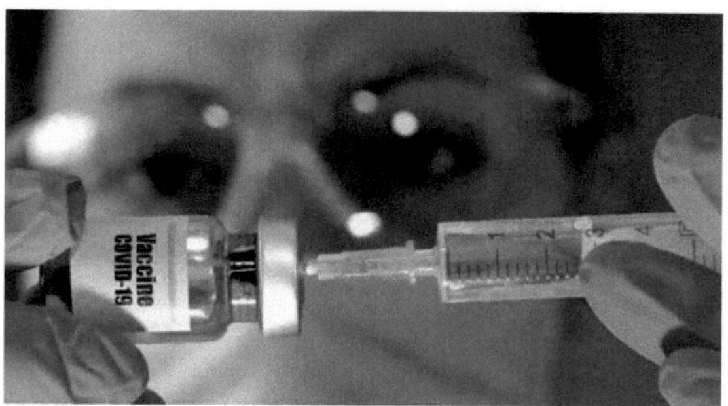

Source: hindustantimes.com

In terms of reducing infectious disease burden, vaccination is only rivaled by clean water (Plotkin and Plotkin 2018, 1-15). There appears to be no viable alternative to a vaccine for mitigating the economic and social impact of COVID-19. As of October 5, 2020, the disease had afflicted over 6 million people and claimed the lives of over 102,000 people in India (Worldometer, 2020). A slew of lockdowns and social distancing measures imposed by union and state governments have been ineffective in containing the disease's spread. With no known treatment options, a massive vaccination campaign to confer herd immunity is a promising path to normalcy.

The natural spread of the disease can be used to build herd immunity instead of mass vaccination.

However, in order to achieve herd immunity, approximately 70% of India's population would have to be infected with COVID-19 (WHO, 2020). With a 1.5 percent assumed mortality rate, the death toll to achieve herd immunity would be an unacceptably high loss of 15 million lives (Mint, 2020). Early preparation is essential for a successful event. Vaccination rollout is thus critical. Over 180 COVID-19 vaccine candidates are currently in various stages of clinical trials around the world. Examinations (Krammer 2020, 1-12). Because of the urgency of the situation, vaccine research has been accelerated and shortened. The development process was reduced from over a decade to a few months (Hanney et al, 2020, 61). A

India, which has a robust vaccine development program, not only plans for domestic manufacture of COVID-19 vaccine but also for its distribution in countries that cannot afford to buy expensive vaccines from the Western world. In India, the data emanating from clinical trials of different vaccines support their eligibility for emergency authorization, even though some of the final details are not available yet. The emphasis now is on the quality control, quality production, and cost control of these vaccines to make them affordable to even the poorest nations in the world.

Background and timeline

In India, free immunization against COVID-19 began on January 16, 2021, and the government is asking all of its inhabitants to get vaccinated as part of what is likely to be the world's largest vaccination programme. Four of the eight COVID-19 vaccines currently undergoing clinical trials in India were created there. Covishield (the Oxford-AstraZeneca vaccine) and Covaxin, a home-grown vaccine produced by Bharat Biotech, have been licensed for limited emergency use by India's medicines authority. Manufacturers in India have said that they will be able to meet the country's future COVID-19 vaccination needs. The workforce and cold-chain infrastructure in place prior to the pandemic are sufficient to vaccinate 30 million healthcare workers in the first instance. The Indian government has taken immediate steps to increase the country's vaccine manufacturing capacity, as well as a computerised system to address and monitor all elements of vaccine administration. Despite the fact that the vaccine is not necessary, India, which has a population of 1380 million people (as of 2020), plans to give it to all of its residents who are willing to take it. Due to India's large population, vaccine importation may not be the best solution. According to the International Air Transport Association (IATA), transporting the vaccine from production sites abroad to distribution areas would necessitate thousands of flights.

Vaccine Development Programme

India, which has a sophisticated vaccine development programme, intends to manufacture the COVID-19 vaccine domestically as well as distribute it to countries that cannot afford to acquire expensive vaccines from the West. COVID-19 vaccine candidates in development and clinical testing in India are among the most advanced products in the world. Apart from the COVID-19 vaccines developed in India, other local pharmaceutical and biotech companies have inked collaboration agreements with vaccine developers from other countries. These cooperation vary from clinical trials through vaccine manufacture and distribution on a wide scale. The following is a list of eight vaccine candidates that are currently being tested in India.

Oxford-AstraZeneca, Codagenix, and Novavax have all struck agreements with the Serum Institute of India (SII) in Pune. It is now mass-producing the Oxford-AstraZeneca Adenovirus vector-based vaccine AZD1222 (also known as "Covishield" in India), and it has roughly 50 million doses on hand. SII plans to increase its capacity to 2 billion doses per year. The Drugs Controller General of India (DCGI) and the Indian Council for Medical Research have granted Covishield a "at-risk manufacturing and stockpiling license" (ICMR). The ICMR funded the clinical trials of the Covishield vaccine developed with the master stock from Oxford-AstraZeneca. The US-based pharma claims that their Covid jab was found to be 89.3% effective in a UK trial.

One of the company's two vaccines is CovaxinTM, India's first indigenous COVID-19 vaccine, developed and manufactured by Bharat Biotech International Limited in conjunction with the National Institute of Virology of the ICMR. CovaxinTM is a virus vaccine that was created in Vero cells. As an adjuvant, the inactivated virus is mixed with Alhydroxiquim-II (Algel-IMDG), a chemosorbed imidazoquinoline onto aluminum hydroxide gel that boosts immune response and provides longer-lasting immunity. A licensing arrangement with Kansas-based ViroVax allows this technology to be deployed.

Cold chain and supply strategies

COVAX Supply ChainTechnical Working Group and National Logistics Working Group A strong supply chain management team is critical for the vaccine introduction. Countries should build on existing committees and working groups already in place to define the COVAX teams but keep in mind that the target groups will be different to those in usual new vaccine introduction activities. It will therefore be necessary to widen the committees to include other relevant stakeholders. Under the guidance of the COVAX National Coordinating Committee (CNCC), the COVAX Technical Working Group (CTWG) and National Logistics Working Group (NLWG) should initiate the following activities:

Assign receiving and acceptance responsibilities to the right entities, such as:

- the regulatory authority bodies within a country, or existing mechanism for importing vaccines; and
- customs agents or national custom authorities.

Secure the system design with the support of the national logistics teams to ensure:

- temporary customs storage; – transportation from the airport to the national stores; – adequate CCE capacity;
- vehicles to transport vaccines safely to all regions and districts with different loading capacities; and – system design team to distribute vaccines within the country.

The composition of and guidance on how to establish a NLWG can be found at: NLWG guide

Strategies adopted by the Indian Government for Vaccines Storage

India has enough capacity to produce vaccines (about 2.4 billion doses per year) as well as medical and surgical disposables such as vials, stoppers, syringes, gauze, and alcohol swabs. The obstacle, however, was the vaccine storage and shipment, which had very particular temperature regimens. Some vaccines being developed and manufactured in other regions of the world require storage temperatures as low as 80 degrees Celsius. Fortunately, the vaccines that India was the first to launch for distribution only require a storage temperature of 2–8 °C.

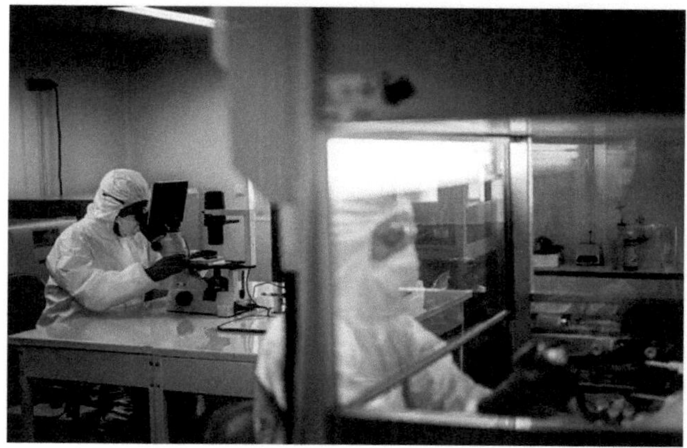

Source: brinknews.com

The government has been working on strategies to ensure that the COVID-19 vaccination is distributed quickly and effectively.

- Vaccine producers have begun airlifting vaccines in cold boxes with digital temperature tags to four large depots in Haryana, Mumbai, Chennai, and Kolkata, where they will be housed in walk-in coolers.
- The vaccines would then be sent to selected stores in 37 states/UTs by flights or insulated vans. The State/UT administrations transport them from these 41 centers to temperature-controlled facilities at district-level vaccination depots.
- Vaccines are kept in ice-lined refrigerators (ILRs) in districts, then transferred to distribution facilities in cold boxes and ultimately to vaccination sites in ice-packed vaccine carriers.

The COVID Vaccine Intelligence Network (Co-WIN) vaccine delivery management system, which is a cloud-based digitalized platform, already monitors the temperature of 29,000 cold-chain locations in real time. The Co-WIN platform was created in India, but it can be used by any country.

For this, the Indian government will provide help.

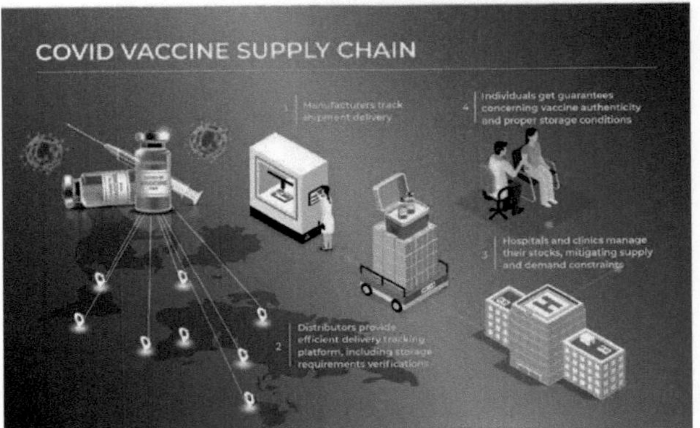

Source: weforum.org

Pfizer India is said to have requested extra time, but the company's mRNA vaccine has already been approved for emergency use in a number of nations, including the United States and the United Kingdom, as well as by the World Health Organization (WHO). Though the extraordinarily low temperature of 70°C required for storing the Pfizer vaccine makes delivery in India difficult, the company has indicated that it will make the appropriate accommodations. However, current Indian rules prohibit the use of any vaccination (such as the Pfizer vaccine) that has not passed adequate clinical testing in India.

The Indian government has established a National Expert Group on COVID-19 Vaccine Administration (NEGVAC) to advise on all aspects of COVID-19 vaccine administration in India19. The COVID-19 vaccination will be administered initially to healthcare workers, frontline workers, and people over 50 (with a preference for those over 60), followed by people under 50 with comorbidities. The government has formed a group of experts from numerous specialties, including oncology, nephrology, pulmonology, and cardiology, to determine the clinical criteria that should be used to prioritise persons with comorbidities for Covid-19 vaccination. After providing some confirmation of identity, eligible persons who have been missed from the rolls for one reason or another will be able to self-register for vaccination. The remaining population will be vaccinated based on disease epidemiology and vaccine availability after over 300 million people were vaccinated in the first wave. The Indian government has arranged for 600 million doses of the COVID-19 vaccine to be procured from the above-mentioned firms and is in the process of negotiating for another billion doses. The government bought Covishield, developed by SII, and Covaxin, produced by Bharat Biotech Ltd, and these were first administered. Nonetheless, as and when the other vaccinations are licensed for delivery after clinical trials, the government may change its strategy. While obtaining the vaccine is the first step, distributing and immunizing the vast Indian population is a major logistical challenge.

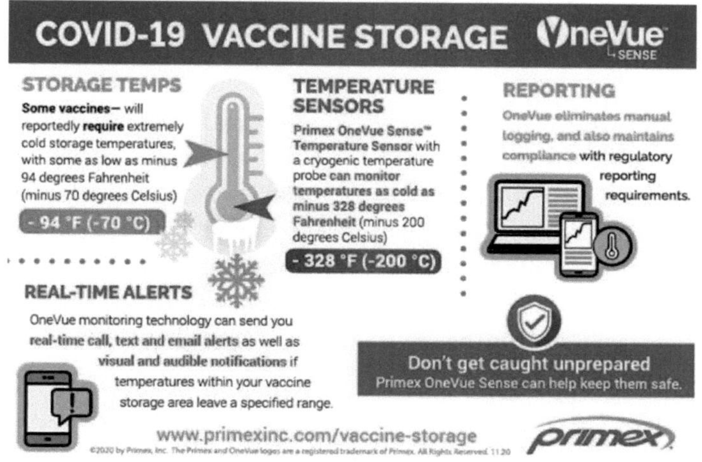

Source: primexinc.com

On November 24, 2020, Indian Prime Minister Shri Narendra Modi met with chief ministers and other representatives from states and union territories to discuss vaccination distribution strategy (UTs). On November 28, 2020, he paid a visit to the three major enterprises to get firsthand knowledge and to assure them of the government's complete support.

Midwives and auxiliary nurse midwives, who have a significantly broader reach in the interiors and rural areas, were included in the first group of health workers educated in vaccination capabilities, since India plans to have COVID-19 immunization campaigns in both urban and rural areas at the same time. These well-trained personnel will play a critical role in rural India's health care. The government intends to enlist the help of allied healthcare professionals such as pharmacists and public health officials in order to broaden a vaccination programme.

Not just in metropolitan areas, but also in rural areas of India, a considerable number of private clinical laboratories, including diagnostic laboratories, have been established. The majority of them have adequate infrastructure and people. Both the government and private clinical laboratories would benefit if they were included in the COVID-19 vaccine program. All of these activities will be carried out under stringent regulatory oversight, with a standard operating procedure (SOP) to guide the trained workers and a standard protocol set by government bodies.

Conclusion

India is in a unique position to provide the globe with affordable medical, surgical, and vital generic medications. India is also well-known for being the world's largest vaccine production and distributor. The present COVID-19 pandemic has resulted in quick development, emergency use authorization, and unprecedented collaboration among numerous parties. Vaccination may be a cost-effective method for people's survival and a higher quality of life, as well as for the resuscitation of India's economy.

References

Krause, P., Fleming, T. R., Longini, I., Henao-Restrepo, A. M., Peto, R., Dean, N. E., ... & Henao-Restrepo, A. M. (2020). COVID-19 vaccine trials should seek worthwhile efficacy. The Lancet, 396(10253), 741-743.

Kochhar, S., & Salmon, D. A. (2020). Planning for COVID-19 vaccines safety surveillance. Vaccine, 38(40), 6194-6198.

https://vaccine.icmr.org.in/covid-19-vaccine

Le, T. T., Cramer, J. P., Chen, R., & Mayhew, S. (2020). Evolution of the COVID-19 vaccine development landscape. Nat Rev Drug Discov, 19(10), 667-668.

Gupta, I., & Baru, R. (2020). Economics & ethics of the COVID-19 vaccine: How prepared are we?. The Indian Journal of Medical Research, 152(1-2), 153.

Rego, G. N., Nucci, M. P., Alves, A. H., Oliveira, F. A., Marti, L. C., Nucci, L. P., ... & Gamarra, L. F. (2020). Current clinical trials protocols and the global effort for immunization against SARS-CoV-2. Vaccines, 8(3), 474.

Wolemonwu, V. C. (2020). Human Challenge Trials for a COVID-19 Vaccine. Voices in Bioethics, 6.

Kumar, V. M., Pandi-Perumal, S. R., Trakht, I., & Thyagarajan, S. P. (2021). Strategy for COVID-19 vaccination in India: the country with the second highest population and number of cases. Npj Vaccines, 6(1), 1-7.

Naik, S., Paleja, A., Mahajan, M., Ramachandran, N., Dixit, S., Matthan, R., ... & Kotasthane, P. (2020). A COVID-19 vaccine deployment strategy for India. *Indian Public Policy Review, 1*(2 (Nov-Dec)), 42-58.

CHAPTER EIGHT

Covid Variants: Emerging Concerns

Introduction

The COVID-19 pandemic has wreaked havoc on health-care systems, forced the closure of schools and towns, and thrown the world into recession. While 2020 was a difficult year, the introduction of numerous forms of the severe acute respiratory syndrome coronavirus 2 in 2021 appears to be even more problematic (SARS-CoV-2). In order to circumvent immunity, the race to vaccinate the entire planet will have to adapt to the pathogen's continual evolution.

Viruses are constantly evolving due to mutation. A variation of the original virus is one that has one or more additional mutations. SARS-CoV-2 (Severe Acute Respiratory Syndrome Coronavirus 2) is a beta coronavirus in the Coronaviridae family. SARS-CoV-2 is a spherical, enclosed virus. Coronaviruses are divided into four genera, with viruses known to cause human disease in the alpha and beta genera. They are zoonotic viruses, meaning they can be passed from one animal to another. COVID-19 is transmitted through droplets, aerosols, and contact with infected surfaces. Air pollutants are also considered to be associated with COVID-19 transmission.

Antigenic drift and antigenic shift are two ways viruses change over time. The SARS-CoV-2 genome is likewise prone to changes that result in antigenic drift and immunological recognition failure. The first reports of double and triple mutant variants in India resulted in a substantial increase in the number of infection. Emerging variants not only increase transmissibility, morbidity, and mortality, but they also have the ability to evade detection by existing or currently available diagnostic tests, potentially delaying diagnosis and treatment, have decreased susceptibility to antivirals, monoclonal antibodies, and convalescent plasma, can cause reinfection in previously infected and recovered individuals, and vaccine breakthrough. The ability of COVID-19 vaccines to protect against infection or sickness caused by these novel SARS-CoV-2 mutations is a significant question.

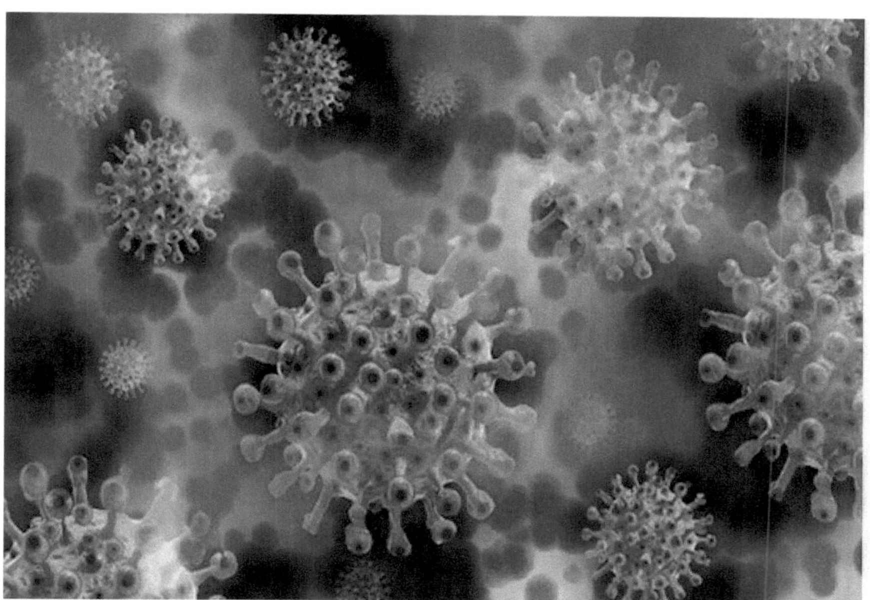

Source: www.ndtv.com

Variants Of Covid 19

SARS-CoV-2 is an RNA virus that can produce a range of strains due to mutation. UV rays, metals, and endogenous components of organisms are all mutagens. In terms of virulence, immunological response in the body, and vaccination efficiency, each strain is unique.

Since September 2020, eight noteworthy SARS-CoV-2 mutations have been discovered:

Alpha

The World Health Organization considers *alpha* to be a variation of concern; alpha was first discovered in Kent, England, in September 2020, and was the catalyst for the UK's second wave. This variation was estimated to be roughly 70% more transmissible than the original at first.

Beta

Beta was first detected in South Africa in May 2020, and the WHO has classified it as a variety of concern. Beta has been linked to a 50 percent increase in transmission by the US Centers for Disease Control and Prevention (CDC), but the real concern is that it appears to be able to avoid several existing vaccines. Although the producer of Sputnik V says that it is "very effective" against beta, at least one study has found that neutralizing efficacy against this variation has decreased.

Gamma

Gamma was first discovered in November 2020 in Manaus, Brazil, and is another variety of worry for WHO. It is still the most common variation in South America at the time of writing. Gamma SARS-CoV-2 is 1.7-2.4 times more transmissible than wild-type SARS-CoV-2, according to research. Few trials have been done to see if Covid vaccinations are effective against the gamma version.

Delta

Delta continues to drive a fast surge of cases throughout much of Asia, including Bangladesh, Iran, Iraq, Japan, Kazakhstan, Malaysia, Myanmar, Pakistan, South Korea, Thailand, and Vietnam14, as well as in India, where it was first identified in October 2020.

According to one study, the delta variation of SARS-CoV-2 is the most transmissible, up to 60% more so than the alpha variant. It's been dubbed a "enhanced" version of the alpha variety, thanks to a mutation that makes it more infective in the airways, according to researchers. This indicates that the virus has multiplied in the sick person, allowing them to discharge more virus into the air. Another issue is that if the delta form is more effective at infecting human airway cells, people could become infected even after receiving less exposure. The Oxford-AstraZeneca vaccine has a 67 percent efficacy against delta, while the Pfizer-BioNTech vaccine has an 88 percent efficacy, according to research, although the manufacturers of Sputnik V say that it is 90 percent efficient against it.

Another development is the advent of delta plus, which is delta with a K417N spike protein mutation. As of the 23rd of July, 45 cases of this type had been reported in England. The Washington Post reported that the delta plus cases were mostly in younger adults, according to Colin Angus, a public health policy modeller and expert.

Eta, Lota, Kappa and Lambda

Although little is known about *Eta*, it has been found in 72 countries, including Nigeria and the United Kingdom, where it was first detected in December 2020. It has been classified as a “variant of interest” by the WHO, which is the second highest level of alert.

Little is known about the *Lota* variety, which has been reported in 53 countries thus far.

Kappa is a variation of interest to WHO, having been first detected in India in October 2020. There have been reports from 55 different nations.

Lambda was discovered in Peru in December 2020 and became the dominant form three months later. It's been found in 41 different nations

News Letter

TRUSTED NEWS SINCE 1737

Sussexes in last appearance as senior Royals

Farmer's friends praise 'tragic young gentleman'

PROVINCE STARTING TO FEEL MAJOR DISRUPTION

Coronavirus: Now it's getting serious

- Belfast St Patrick's Day parade cancelled
- Another local footballer positive
- Schools closed for deep clean

Source: www.bbc.com

Deadly Fungus

In India, the second wave of COVID-19 has resulted in a rise in cases, a reduction in crucial treatment supplies, and an increase in mortality, particularly among the young.

Many cases of mucormycosis, often known as the black fungus, were documented in patients with diabetes and COVID-19, as well as those recovering from infection, during the second wave in India. The onset of an opportunistic fungal infection was caused by the overuse of steroids in the treatment of COVID-19, as well as the virus's immunosuppression. Although cases of black fungus were detected during the first wave, the second wave has become more prevalent in several Indian cities, prompting state governments to designate it an epidemic as well. The Indian Ministry of Health had registered 28 252 instances of black fungus as of June 7, 2021. The white fungus Aspergillosis, which is thought to be far more deadly than the black fungus, is also on the rise, with cases reported in India. As the situation unfolds, it's worth noting that while everyone looked to be at equal danger of becoming infected with the virus, people's ability to sustain and resist infection differed. Patients infected with SARS-CoV-2 in the first wave were mostly over 60 years old, and those with concomitant illnesses were at higher risk of mortality. Surprisingly, younger persons appear to be more susceptible to infection during this latest cycle, and many patients, including those aged 25 to 50, have died at a young age.

Another finding made during the peak of the second wave was that some patients' oxygen saturation dropped suddenly, even while they were recovering well, allowing for less time for proper ventilation assistance. Patients and family members were fearful and worried since it was unclear whether the patients would survive the viral illness, even if they were exhibiting indications of recovery. One explanation could be the occurrence of many SARS-CoV-2 strains that infect people at the same time, with some versions being more pathogenic than others.

The last two years have been difficult and trying, but life goes on. Vaccines do a good job of mitigating the disease, including the existing varieties, but there is no silver bullet in sight when it comes to treatment. The most serious threat in the future would be the recurrent appearance of highly altered varieties like the Omicron.

Omicron: Variant Of Concern

According to WHO sources, the first verified Omicron infection was discovered in a specimen obtained on November 9, 2021. It was classified as VUM by the WHO and given the designation Omicron variant. In mid-November 2021, the novel OMICRON variant was discovered for the first time in South Africa's Gauteng area. The excellent genome sequencing infrastructure in South Africa allows for early detection and reporting of novel variants to the rest of the world. The OMICRON version has already appeared in 77 countries as of December 15, 2021.

RNA viruses are known for their ability to rapidly mutate and change in order to adapt to and survive in changing surroundings. The constellation of more than 50 mutations in the OMICRON variation, of which roughly 30 mutations are in the spike protein, is the most worrying feature.

As the omicron form has grown in popularity in a number of countries, the demand for boosters has increased. Prior to the advent of the omicron type, countries with excellent vaccination programmes used evidence that demonstrated a decline in vaccine effectiveness against infection and clinical illness. The efficacy of COVID-19 vaccines is diminishing, and a new variant, Omicron, has arisen, boosting the risk of another infection outbreak in India. Mass vaccination has been achieved to a large extent in the highly populated country, and is currently being applied, following a number of control procedures. India was hit by a big second wave of infection in April-June 2021, primarily due to delta fluctuation, and a third wave is expected in the near future, necessitating effective management strategies. Due to the discovery of new varieties or the loosening of social distance regulations, daily new occurrences could reach 250k by March 2022, with second-dose effectiveness declining to 50% in the future.

A combination of vaccination and regulated confinement or social isolation is the best way to deal with the current situation and the months ahead. During a pandemic, early diagnosis and quarantine are also critical components in minimising virus transmission. The public has displayed widespread contempt for the 'Covid Appropriate Behaviours,' or CAB, and the masks used vary in quality. N-95 masks are not frequently utilised in India due to their higher costs; instead, the majority of the population utilises either indigenous textile masks or the same, worn-out masks again and over. Because the chaos appears to have no end in sight, the population must learn to live with it in the safest and most secure manner possible.

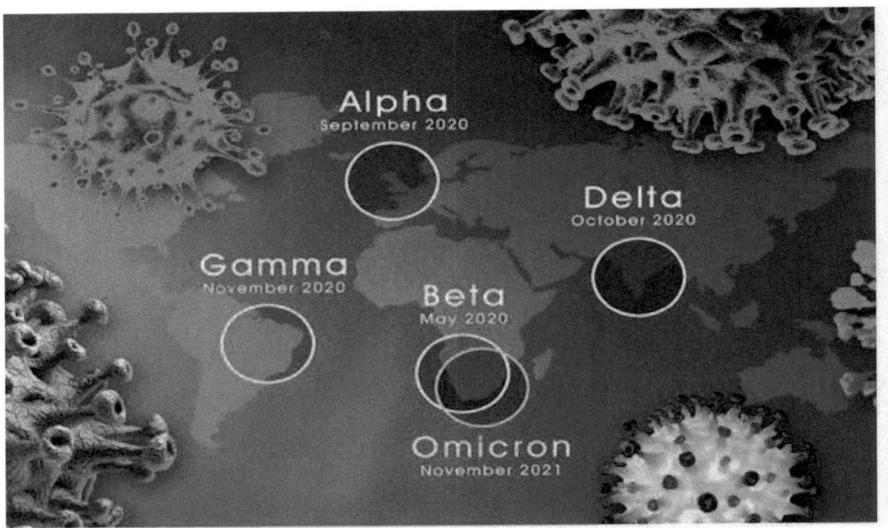

Source: www.the-scientist.com

Conclusion

In the aftermath of its introduction, the origin, transmission capability, and immune-escape potential of the Omicron type remain unknown. It's also unknown whether other Omicron-based variations may appear in the future. As a result, the only method to stop the pandemic is to distribute vaccines that are effective against circulating variants globally. A number of crucial activities are required as a result of the emergence of novel SARS-CoV-2 subtypes. This condition can only be attained through a combination of non-pharmaceutical means and vaccine scale-up until population immunity is obtained, both of which are crucial. Vaccines must be widely available, affordable, and easily accessible throughout the world.

References

Vasireddy, D., Vanaparthy, R., Mohan, G., Malayala, S. V., & Atluri, P. (2021). Review of COVID-19 variants and COVID-19 vaccine efficacy: what the clinician should know?. Journal of Clinical Medicine Research, 13(6), 317.

Fontanet, A., Autran, B., Lina, B., Kieny, M. P., Karim, S. S. A., & Sridhar, D. (2021). SARS-CoV-2 variants and ending the COVID-19 pandemic. The

Lancet, 397(10278), 952-954.

Roy, B., Dhillon, J. K., Habib, N., & Pugazhandhi, B. (2021). Global variants of COVID-19: Current understanding. Journal of Biomedical Sciences, 8(1), 8-11.

Tang, L., Liu, M., Ren, B., Chen, J., Liu, X., Wu, X., ... & Tian, J. (2022). Transmission in home environment associated with the second wave of COVID-19 pandemic in India. Environmental research, 204, 111910.

Mahase, E. (2021). Covid-19: How many variants are there, and what do we know about them?. BMJ, 374.

Kang, G. (2022). SARS-CoV2 vaccine boosters for India. Indian Journal of Medical Microbiology.

Sivadas, N. A., Mahajan, A., & Panda, P. (2021). Control Strategies for the Third wave of COVID-19 infection in India: A Mathematical Model Incorporating Vaccine Effectiveness. medRxiv.

Abhilash, K. P. P. (2021). Alpha, delta and now Omicron: When will the COVID-19 pandemic end?. Current Medical Issues, 19(4), 221.

He, X., Hong, W., Pan, X., Lu, G., & Wei, X. (2021). SARS-CoV-2 Omicron variant: characteristics and prevention. MedComm.

Jain, V. K., Iyengar, K. P., & Vaishya, R. (2021). Differences between First wave and Second wave of COVID-19 in India. Diabetes & Metabolic Syndrome.

Asrani, P., Eapen, M. S., Hassan, M. I., & Sohal, S. S. (2021). Implications of the second wave of COVID-19 in India. The Lancet Respiratory Medicine, 9(9), e93-e94.

Thakur, V., & Kanta Ratho, R. (2021). OMICRON (B. 1.1. 529): A new SARS-CoV-2 Variant of Concern mounting worldwide fear. Journal of medical virology.

CHAPTER NINE

Covid-19 Vaccine: India's Plans And Deployment Strategies

Introduction

"People's Vaccine for India: No one is safe until everyone is safe"

It's been a year since the first instance of new coronavirus infections was discovered in Wuhan, China. During the early stages of the epidemic, the focus was on preventing and reducing transmission.

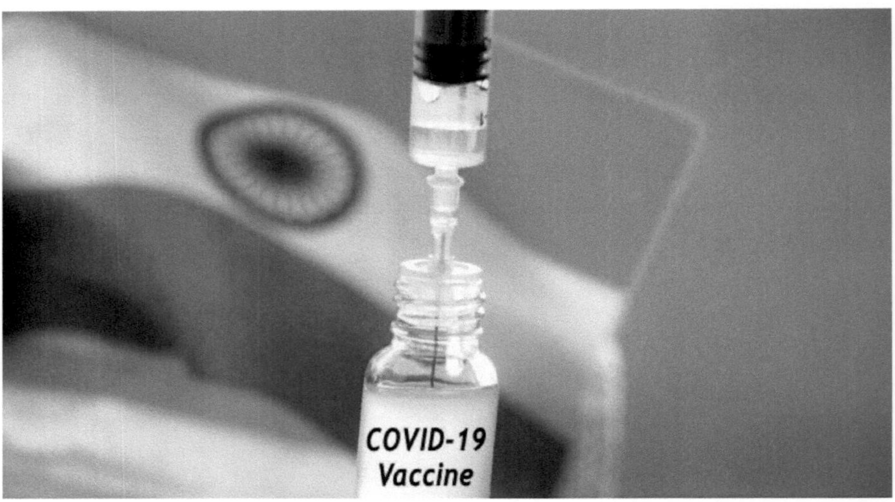

Source :orfonline.org

On the 16th of January 2021, India started administering COVID-19 vaccinations. The Oxford–AstraZeneca vaccine (marketed as Covishield by Serum Institute of India) and Covaxin were first authorised in India (a vaccine developed locally by Bharat Biotech). Sputnik V (manufactured under licence by Dr. Reddy's Laboratories, with additional production starting in September from Serum Institute of India), Moderna vaccines, Johnson & Johnson vaccine, ZyCoV-D (a vaccine locally developed by Zydus Cadila), and other vaccine candidates undergoing local clinical trials have since joined individuals.

In January 2021, India launched Vaccine Maitri (Vaccine Friendship), a humanitarian project aimed at leveraging the country's pharmaceutical sector to sell Indian-made vaccinations to other countries. Since January 20, India has donated over 5.5 million vaccines to neighbouring countries such as Bahrain, Bangladesh, Bhutan, Maldives, Mauritius, Myanmar, Nepal, Seychelles, and Sri Lanka, according to the Ministry of External Affairs. The country also plans to send doses to Africa, Nicaragua, Oman, the Caribbean Community, and the COVAX programme, as well as distribute vaccines to other countries through commercial exports.

Modelling vaccination scenarios, exploring approaches to reach children at risk, and co-optimizing vaccination tactics for societal and individual benefit in simultaneously are all part of optimising vaccine deployment for India.

India had provided approximately 1.10 billion doses of vaccinations, including first and second doses of presently licenced vaccines, as of November 10, 2021. Nine months after the vaccine was introduced in India, over half of the eligible population had gotten at least one injection, with 19% receiving both.

The Indian government has taken immediate steps to increase the country's vaccine manufacturing capacity, as well as developing a comprehensive digital system to manage and monitor all elements of vaccine delivery.

Objectives

- To review and study India's prospects for the Covid 19 vaccination.
- To get insight into the Covid 19 vaccine's deployment blueprint in India.

Analysis and Discussion

1. India's prospects for the Covid 19 vaccination

The government has responded to ensure that the vaccination is available to the public. It must have a thorough, time-bound, and transparent COVID-19 Vaccine strategy and action plan developed in conjunction with the states, India's specialists, and the general public, and guarantee openness in government-pharmaceutical contracting arrangements. Providing ethical and safe vaccination access to everyone would save lives, relieve strain on the healthcare system, and speed India's return to normality. In the shortest amount of time, India must dramatically increase immunization, particularly for the most vulnerable.

The government is also attempting to expand the number of Covid-19 immunization sites by utilizing its complete network of 1 lakh child immunization centers, which are primarily located in rural regions. Around the mid-July or August, the Centre plans to put Covid-19 vaccination on a "mission mode," aiming for an average of around 1 crore inoculations per day, as vaccine supplies are expected to improve, with not only the Serum Institute of India (SII) and Bharat Biotech producing more doses, but also local production and supplies of Sputnik V likely to begin.

India, which has a sophisticated vaccine development programme, intends to make COVID-19 vaccine domestically as well as distribute it to nations that cannot afford to acquire expensive vaccines from the West. Even if some of the final details are not yet available, evidence from clinical studies of many vaccines in India supports their eligibility for emergency authorization. The focus today is on quality control, production quality, and cost management for these vaccinations in order to make them accessible to even the world's poorest countries.

India had provided approximately 1.11 billion doses in total as of November 12, 2021, including the first and second doses of currently licensed vaccinations. Nine months after the vaccine was introduced in India, over half of the eligible population had gotten at least one injection, and 19% had had both.

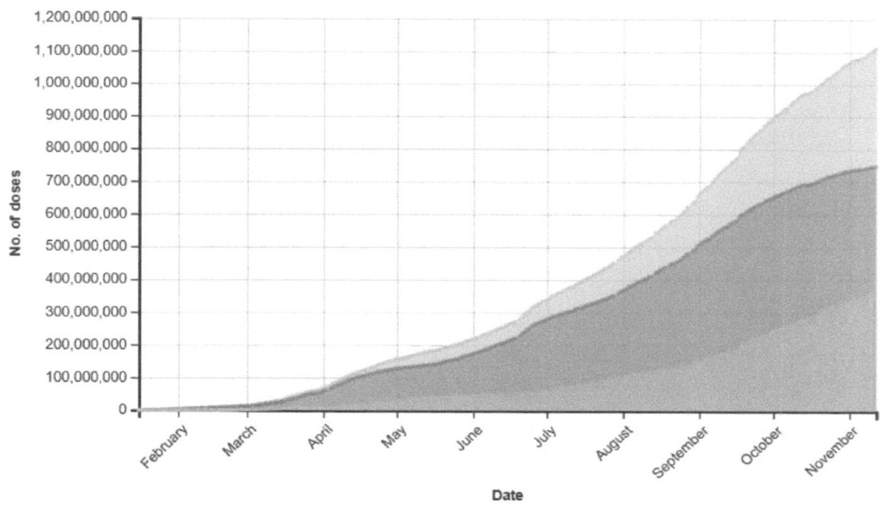

Source:wikipedia.org

Graph of cumulative doses administered across the country

"Total vaccination doses administered across the country"

"Vaccinated (1st dose only)"

"Fully vaccinated"

How Has The Government Determined Who Will Get The Vaccine And When?

According to the Ministry of Health and Family Welfare of the Indian government, the country's national COVID-19 vaccine policy was based on a methodical and scientific approach that prioritized immunization of more vulnerable or high-risk populations. There were three stages to the immunization campaign.

- The first phase, which began on January 16, 2021, aimed to immunize healthcare and frontline personnel.
- The second phase, which began on March 1, 2021, was split into two halves. People over the age of sixty and those over the age of forty-five with particular comorbidities were vaccinated during the first portion. The administration agreed on April 1, 2021, to extend eligibility to anybody above the age of 45.

- The third phase started on May 1, 2021, and anybody above the age of eighteen may get vaccinated. The immunization rates are listed here as of May 15, 2021.

1. **Deployment blueprint in India**

Obtaining sufficient vaccine supplies and successfully deploying the vaccine to India's 1.3 billion people is a tremendous administrative and logistical undertaking. On the side of the economy, if 80% of India's population is vaccinated, a billion individuals must be vaccinated. The necessity to track the time between two doses and convey it to recipients adds another degree of complication to the majority of the existing vaccination options. In comparison, India's existing Universal Immunization Programme (UIP) provides free vaccinations to approximately 27 million youngsters and 30 million expectant mothers each year. As a result, the COVID-19 vaccination must reach one billion individuals, which is roughly 16 times the number of people who receive the UIP vaccine each year. In its current form, even India's well-oiled and effective UIP machinery will be unable to complete the COVID-19 immunization exercise in a timely manner. To ensure timely and efficient distribution of the vaccination, new administrative systems are required.

While a result, even as researchers anticipate for the vaccine to be approved following clinical trials, an all-India deployment requires prior preparation to guarantee infrastructure is in place, capabilities are established, and receivers are ready.

Given the magnitude of the situation and the implications at risk, India must act quickly to guarantee that its citizens are properly vaccinated. By December 2021, experts suggest that India vaccinate 80% of its people, at a cost of 50,000-250,000 crores.

Estimating vaccine demand, securing supply, choosing delivery channels, and conducting post-market surveillance are the four stages of the vaccination activity planning process.

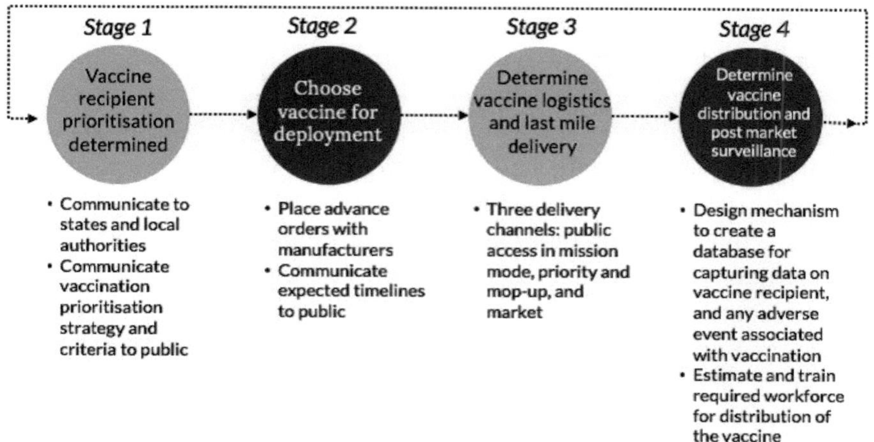

Source :TI_Vaccine+Deployment

The quick and widespread implementation of a COVID-19 vaccination is a huge undertaking. By December 2021, 80 percent of India's population should have been vaccinated, thanks to a well-defined plan and staggered, decentralized distribution. This will involve Indian government investment and fast action, as well as business sector engagement and open communication with the general population. India's potential to produce low-cost, reliable vaccines should be exploited. In addition, India should leverage its existing processes to control administrative activities, engage in health worker training, and establish a rigorous and open post-market surveillance capacity to track vaccination success.

Recommendations and Findings

- Each vaccine producer must announce the price of vaccination doses for private hospitals, and any further modifications is then communicated ahead of time. Service prices in private hospitals can be as high as Rupees 150 each dosage. The price being charged may be monitored by state governments.
- Vaccination is compulsory for all residents, regardless of their financial situation. People who can easily afford it are urged to visit a private hospital's immunization clinic.

- Every person may schedule vaccination appointments using the CoWIN platform in a simple and secure manner. In order to minimize any inconvenience to citizens, both government and private vaccination centers may provide an onsite registration facility, which would be available for both individuals and groups of individuals, and for which a detailed procedure would be finalized and published by States/UTs.
- States may also make the best use of Common Service Centers and Call Centers to let residents schedule appointments ahead of time.
- India should make immunization certificates mandatory for all citizens, regardless of age, when traveling and participating in all forms of entertainment.
- The government must act to guarantee that the vaccination is available to the general public. It must have a thorough, time-bound, and transparent COVID-19 Vaccine strategy and action plan developed in consultation with the states, India's specialists, and the general public, as well as ensuring openness in government-pharmaceutical contracting arrangements.

Conclusion

The conclusion of this perspective was to emphasize the central importance of vaccine development and immunization strategies used during a pandemic in a highly populated country (India). This study may be used as a baseline for future pandemic preparedness, as well as to adapt and refine strategies that will benefit the general public.

Anti-covid vaccines have received favorable responses from over 80% of India's population. In India, vaccination apprehension is among the lowest in the world. In the early months of 2021, there remained vaccination apprehension, particularly in rural India and among underprivileged and tribal groups. Vaccine apprehension was greatly reduced as a result of constant government and public awareness. More than half of the daily dosages delivered in India have come from rural areas since May 2021. In India, a high number of individuals want to acquire the covid vaccination, resulting in overpopulation and mismanagement in vaccine clinics.

As of November 12, 2021, India had administered around 1.11 billion doses in aggregate, along with the first and second doses of currently approved vaccines. Nearly half of the potential Indian population have received at least one shot within nine months after the immunization has been introduced, and 19 percent had received both.

Bibliography

- (2021). Retrieved from Revised Guidelines for implementation of National: https://www.mohfw.gov.in/pdf/RevisedVaccinationGuidelines.pdf
- Dey, S. (2021). Covid-19: Government plans 1 crore daily vaccines from middl .. Retrieved from https://timesofindia.indiatimes.com/india/covid-19-government-plans-1-crore-daily-vaccines-from-middle-of-july/articleshow/83127681.cms
- India, O. (2021). People's Vaccine for India: No one is safe until everyone is safe. Retrieved from https://www.oxfamindia.org/petition/peoples-vaccine-india-no-one-safe-until-everyone-safe?gclid=Cj0KCQiAsqOMBhDFARIsAFBTN3dMjyCfaZ1K
- x4N2XIozJM_3OKFAHAcFdsFxWRtzTL55yFgBOSCE0NgaAp65EALw_wcB
- JOSEPH, A. K. (2021). What Is Happening to India's COVID-19 Vaccine Program? Retrieved from https://carnegieindia.org/2021/05/19/what-is-happening-to-india-s-covid-19-vaccine-program-pub-84570
- OOMMEN C. KURIAN, K. K. (2021). The Himalayan Challenge: India's quest to achieve herd immunity through vaccination. Retrieved from https://www.orfonline.org/expert-speak/himalayan-challenge-india-quest-achieve-herd-immunity-vaccination/
- Shambhavi Naik, A. P. (2020). A COVID-19 Vaccine Deployment Strategy for India. Retrieved from https://ippr.in/index.php/ippr/article/view/20
- Velayudhan Mohan Kumar, S. R.-P. (2021). Strategy for COVID-19 vaccination in India: the country with the second highest population and number of cases. Retrieved from https://www.nature.com/articles/s41541-021-00327-2
- Wikipedia. (2021). COVID-19 vaccination in India. Retrieved from https://en.wikipedia.org/wiki/COVID-19_vaccination_in_India

CHAPTER TEN

Covid Vaccine Challenges in Containing the Epidemic

Abstract

The coronovirus disease , Covid 19, as a pandemic shook the world health care system and economy to such an extent that the epidemic is still spreading and showing no signs of decreasing trend. This pandemic is a dangerous syndrome because it is showing every decade in different forms, such as Severe Acute Respiratory Syndrome (SARS) in 2002, Middle East Respiratory Syndrome (MERS) in 2012 and now Covid 19, Similar epidemics are expected in future also, and this epidemic is changing in unpredictable forms. Thus, the world as such has to face new challenges and issues over time. This article highlights some challenges of containing the coronovirus Covid 19.

Keywords: Covid 19, Vaccination, Challenges, SARS, MERS

Introduction

We are all aware of the breakdown of the Covid, and how India and the world developed strategies to overcome the spread and contain the coronavirus. A large number of people across the world were affected by the virus, and slowly India was also on the verge of acquiring the epidemic. The Indian government also took drastic measures to contain the spread of the coronovirus. As the spread was very rapid, many people were affected and diagnosed with Covid positive symptoms. Studies showed that the Covid positive test was linked to fatigue, mental illness and sleep issues. A new study by Business Standard on coronovirus, confirms that people who tested positive (confirmed by PCR-test) had a risk of high fatigue, mental illness and sleep problems. The study showed that there was an 83 percent increase in mental illness in people, following a positive PCR-test. This was due to pandemic-related anxieties. As fatigue increased due to sleep disorders and persisted due to an increase in anxieties of developing a positive symptom. People stayed indoors in houses, and this was also a cause of increased mental illness due to lack of communication and mobility, due to imposition of lockdown. As lockdown was imposed, throughout the nation and the world, people became anxious and developed fear in them about a possible infection. Children and old age people were the most affected population. People became wary of health issues and people with comorbidities had other health issues, which further aggravated their sufferings and mental illness. As lockdown persisted, financial issues in families cropped up due to job loss and death in the families. As families experienced more stress, the positivity rate increased, and shifting to a hospital and acquiring a bed became a major problem. People had to wait for treatment in hospitals and as the demand increased for procuring beds in hospitals, corruption prevailed and the fear of losing their near and dear ones further aggravated the situation. Cities, towns, and nations experienced a lot of chaos and hostility due to the lack of proper care and the lack of training of health care workers due to improper planning and handling. People feared acquiring a positive symptom. Affordable people used private hospitals for treatment and the less deprived perished due to no financial resources.

India's unusual Covid vaccine problem

Hospitals across the country experienced a shortage of trained health care workers, doctors, and medicines. Even at the planning level, people had to search for the availability of essentials like medicines, ventilators, beds, oxygen, etc. The government of all the nations supported the researchers and pharmacy industries in finding a solution in developing vaccines and medicines to contain the coronavirus. India also developed its own vaccines to administer to its people and also exported it to other countries. Containing the pandemic of coronavirus was a challenge. People had to wait for a few weeks to show signs of recovery. Immunity-boosting medicines prevailed till a vaccine was developed.

Approval and acceptance of vaccines by the government took its own time, till a regulatory was issued. The government had to woo the researchers, investors, and industrialists to develop a vaccine in a record time with minimal cost and buy-back agreement. Researchers had to work day and night in developing a good vaccine. Trial runs on patients were conducted before administering as a drug in hospitals. Developing, distribution and dissemination, deployment were the major issues faced by many countries and pharmaceutical companies. Deployment of personnel to administer vaccines was another hurdle due to the shortage of trained health care workers. People had to run around for health centers and approved hospitals to get themselves tested and also to get vaccinated. India was the second-largest affected country in the world for coronovirus, but much went without any reporting.

As India rolled out one of the world's biggest inoculation programmes, some health care workers and frontline workers were hesitating because of safety. When most of the world was struggling to get vaccines for inoculation, India had the opposite problem, 'Plenty of shots, but a shortage of people to take them. Vaccine hesitancy among Indian population is prevailing even now. Unless, the inoculation rate increases, India will fall short of its target of inoculating people to its mark. As Indian population became weary and hesitant, additional health care workers and counselors had to be deployed to carry out the vaccination project. Many traveled to different villages and to their houses and convince people about its benefits and advantages.

Only, a small percentage of people are really fearful of a possible relapse and the possibility of a third wave. Our minds are full of agony and cannot forget the last year's pandemic which had shattered people's confidence and brought about an economic downslide in the country. People are aware of the problems the pandemic had brought in the first and second waves and its implications on society. The sufferings have made them sustainable and have brought about a change in their attitudes. But, this is not enough. They have to follow strict guidelines and take precautionary measures to avert a possible third wave.

The effect of lockdown increased the prices of commodities and motor fuel. The common man faced a lot of difficulties financially and health issues and the possibility of near-normal situations. Job loss has made more people depend on families for assistance and care. Work from a home model has made people more stressful and long working hours put their health at risk.

Low vaccination rates

In India, vaccine hesitation has led to low vaccination rates and has affected the speed of getting a vaccination. Hospitals are in a situation and are unaware of the policy framework regarding unused vaccines and their administration. As of today, people are ill-informed about vaccine effectiveness and its life in the human body. Some common people are of the opinion of taking a booster dose to avoid acquiring the disease and possible relapse. As such, clarity in this matter is required and possible ambiguities among people have to be rested and issuing proper guidelines. Study papers have to be developed among researchers and pharmacy companies, and results have to be announced. Large-scale study papers are necessary to make a proper policy and framework. People should be motivated and instructed to follow proper safety measures, to reduce the spread of the coronavirus. Families play a major role to follow and implement proper health care practices without compromising time and money.

Conclusion

Containment of coronovirus is the need of the hour and is an issue and challenge. The whole society should fight collectively as a main priority. The attitudes and mindset of the people should change and accept the conditions of living and of the workplace as the new normal.

References

1] Business Standard special issue on coronovirus, Nov.2020.

2] National Library of Medicine, National Centre for Biotechnology Information, Sep.2020.

CHAPTER ELEVEN

Distribution Process of COVID-19 Vaccine

Introduction

What Is the Goal of This Strategy?

The report to Congress outlines a strategy for achieving Operation Warp Speed's main goal and objective: assuring that every American who wants a COVID-19 vaccine can get one, starting in January 2021, by delivering safe and effective vaccine doses to the American people.

OWS's leadership has pledged to be open and honest with Congress, the media, and the American public. OWS has delivered regular briefings to Congress and the media on subjects of relevance and will continue to do so when the organization reaches new milestones. Congress has played a critical role in the nation's reaction to the COVID19 outbreak.

OWS has made significant progress toward a safe and effective COVID-19 vaccine, with many candidates in Phase 3 clinical trials, thanks to emergency supplemental and flexible discretionary financing. Simultaneously, OWS and its partners are working on a strategy to provide a safe and effective product to Americans as soon as feasible. Experts from the Department of Health and Human Services (HHS) are directing vaccine development, while experts from the Department of Defense (DoD) are coordinating vaccine supply, production, and distribution with the Centers for Disease Control and Prevention (CDC) and other elements of HHS.

The nationwide COVID-19 immunization program involves meticulous coordination between the federal, state, local, tribal, and territory governments, as well as a wide range of public and corporate partners. Cooperation has already begun on each of these fronts, as highlighted throughout this strategy document.

What is the Strategy?

Once a vaccine has been approved or authorized by the FDA, there are four critical steps to complete in order to meet the primary goal of assuring vaccination availability to every American who desires it:

- Continue to work with state, tribal, territorial, and local partners, as well as other stakeholders and the general public, to disseminate public health information about the vaccine, both before and after it is distributed, and to increase vaccine confidence and uptake.
- Using a transparently defined, phased allocation mechanism, distribute vaccinations as soon as an Emergency Use Authorization/ Biologics License Application is granted.
- Ensure that the vaccine is administered safely and that administration supplies are available.
- Using an information technology (IT) system capable of supporting and tracking distribution, administration, and other relevant data, keep track of the necessary data from the vaccination programme.

Distribution

What is required: - A distribution plan must be able to deliver vaccines to all conceivable administration endpoints as soon as FDA authorization or licensure is granted, while staying flexible enough to handle a variety of circumstances such as fluctuating product requirements, manufacturing timetables and volumes. Any distribution operation must assure product safety, maintain control and visibility, manage uptake and acceptability, ensure product traceability, and maximize coverage, all of which necessitate a centralized solution and close local connections.

What we are doing: - The federal government, the 64 jurisdictions with which the CDC works (all 50 states, six localities and territories, and freely associated states), Tribes, industry partners, and other groups are drafting a cooperative strategy for centralized distribution that will be implemented in phases.

There are three main components to distribution:

- Partnerships with state, local, tribal, territorial, and federal health agencies, territories, Tribes, and federal bodies to allocate and distribute vaccinations, with direct distribution to commercial partners.
- A centralized distributor contract with the option of adding backup distributors for extra storage and handling.

- A web-based IT vaccination monitoring system that is adaptable, scalable, and secure for ongoing vaccine allocation, ordering, uptake, and management.

Sate, Trible and partnership: -

The CDC is collaborating with state, municipal, and tribal health departments to improve vaccine distribution and administration plans. CDC has worked with these partners for decades, including through cooperative agreements, to ensure that public health systems have the plans, trained personnel, strategic relationships and partnerships, data systems, and other resources necessary to maintain a successful routine immunization infrastructure, and these plans will be adapted for this vaccine programme.

As part of the Coronavirus Aid, Relief, and Economic Security (CARES) Act and the Families First Coronavirus Response Act, the CDC has provided money to vaccination programmes to help them begin planning for vaccine distribution and delivery. The money will go toward improving staffing, communication, and stakeholder involvement, as well as pandemic preparedness and mass vaccination.

Five pilot jurisdictions—California, Florida, Minnesota, North Dakota, and Philadelphia—have worked with a multi-agency federal team to use a basic plan for administration and alter it to produce jurisdiction-specific plans that will serve as templates for other jurisdictions. Collaboration with federal institutions in their jurisdiction, coordination with national chain partners, vaccination of vital work forces, and reaching marginalized communities will all be part of jurisdiction planning.

With CDC's technical assistance, each jurisdiction will be expected to construct a "micro plan" based on their existing plans as well as the results from the first five jurisdictions supported. These micro plans will identify vaccination locations and logistical considerations, as well as how the sites will be integrated into the required IT system. As additional information about the precise qualities of the vaccines becomes known, the micro plans will need to be adaptable to allow for adaptability.

Jurisdictions will subsequently integrate providers to the IT system and identify and arrange for the necessary immunization workforce under their cooperative agreements with the CDC, under which CARES Act awards were granted. Jurisdictions will also be in charge of setting the framework for vaccinating high-risk and priorities populations through various outreach activities, such as forming a workgroup or stakeholder groups and forming a vaccination committee.

Jurisdictions will be expected to include vaccine distribution planning in their micro plans for members of Tribes. In addition, the CDC and OWS are collaborating with the Indian Health Service (IHS) to develop a plan for direct IHS vaccination distribution to Tribes who want it.

Centralized Distribution

The government has full sight, control, and power to transfer assets and use data to enhance vaccine uptake with centralized distribution. CDC announced their centralized distributor contract on August 14 by activating an existing contract option with McKesson, which distributed the H1N1 vaccination during the 2009–2010 H1N1 pandemic. McKesson's current contract, which was won in 2016 after a competitive bidding process, contains a provision for vaccine delivery in the case of a pandemic.

McKesson will supply a certain volume of vaccine to a designated place once vaccines have been allotted to a given authority or authorized partner. In many cases, delivery venues will also be vaccination administration sites. Vaccines can also be provided to locations within jurisdictions, where they will be disseminated to administration sites within health department networks. Vaccines can also be transported to places that are part of national retail pharmacy networks, where they will be distributed to individual pharmacies.

To satisfy demand, this system will be scalable. Some vaccines that require ultra-cold storage may be transported directly from the manufacturer to the administration sites, but this centralized system will handle all distribution.

The McKesson contract can cover the rapid distribution of doses of refrigerated (2–8 degrees Celsius) and frozen (-20 degrees Celsius) vaccinations if necessary.

The Crisis

The Covid-19 issue has thrown everyday life into disarray, wreaking havoc on healthcare institutions, the global economy, and people's lives. Covid-19 has been linked to 175.5 million confirmed cases worldwide and has claimed the lives of about 3.8 million people. It has shown an increasing number of worldwide social and economic disparities that disproportionately affect low-income and historically marginalized people. Extreme poverty rates have risen dramatically in the last year, and many believe that the situation will only worsen if the threat persists. According to the World Bank, Covid-19 drove between 88 million and 115 million people into extreme poverty in 2020, with an expected growth of 23–35 million individuals in 2021.

This has exacerbated world hunger, with an estimated 155 million people facing acute food insecurity by the year 2020. Covid-19 is also wreaking havoc on ongoing public health programmes by diverting resources away from non-pandemic pharmaceutical development, disrupting routine immunizations, and wreaking havoc on public health infrastructure.

As rates of extreme poverty, children out of school, and other factors rise, progress toward broader development goals, such as the Sustainable Development Goals (SDGs), has slowed. The UN High-Level Political Forum in July will focus on recovery from Covid-19 and its implications for the SDGs. The pandemic has also triggered one of the worst global recessions in history, and governments all over the world are still grappling with how to deliver effective relief to their citizens. According to the International Monetary Fund, the global economy would decrease by 3.3 percent in 2020, affecting employment rates, job security, and the flow of international remittances.

Furthermore, the pandemic will have long-term repercussions on children and students, as school closures have touched about 1.5 billion children and youth across 160 nations, including and notably migrant and refugee children.

According to UNICEF, one out of every seven children (214 million worldwide) has "lost more than three-quarters of their in-person learning." School closures are also posing a greater threat to girls‘ education, with the UN projecting that over 11 million girls and young women are at risk of never returning to school as a result of the ongoing crisis.

Administration Priorities

Domestic vaccine distribution was one of the major priorities for the Biden-Harris government when it entered office in January 2021. The administration’s ability to roll out vaccines quickly and effectively across the country provides vital lessons for global vaccine supply chain distribution.

President Biden published a Countrywide Strategy for the Covid-19 Response and Pandemic Preparedness shortly after assuming office, which includes $20 billion to support a national immunization effort. Biden took numerous initiatives to improve manufacturing and delivery in order to meet—and eventually double—his lofty target of giving 100 million shots in the first 100 days. By prioritizing federal government demands in the supply chain and enlisting 1,000 military soldiers to assist his vaccination efforts, he exploited the Defense Production Act (DPA) to speed up production. The government was able to speed up this procedure by simplifying access to the essential equipment, machinery, and supplies through the DPA.

The enormous challenge of producing effective vaccinations to combat Covid-19 has been addressed. Pre-purchase agreements, for example, assist alleviate vaccine makers' worries and ensure sufficient production in the short term. However, with over 12 billion vaccine doses expected to be manufactured by the end of 2021, distribution issues will become a medium-to-long-term priority. These include the transportation industry's slow recovery and the necessity to maintain a temperature-controlled "cold chain" for vaccines. The cost of distribution in the United States has so far been $27 per dose. This will be a substantial burden on developing countries in the search for herd immunity. It is the moral thing to do to ensure that everyone in the globe is immunised, regardless of nationality or financial status. There are additional geostrategic and national security incentives to encourage the deployment of the Covid-19 vaccination in poor countries. The world is not safe until everyone is safe, especially in light of new varieties. At any scale smaller than the entire world, it is impossible to establish and sustain a fully vaccinated bubble. This is a once-in-a-lifetime situation that will necessitate unprecedented global cooperation and bilateral cooperation. It is difficult to cure the domestic economy in the United States without simultaneously healing the global economy. The International Chamber of Commerce forecasts that if vaccinations are not made available to LMICs, the world economy will lose $9.2 trillion dollars. The restoration of the United States' worldwide position is one of the Biden-Harris administration's top priorities, and assisting with vaccine distribution is a critical opportunity to reclaim US leadership.

References

- https://www.hhs.gov/.../strategy-for-distributing-covid-19-vaccine.pdf/
- https://www.hhs.gov/coronavirus/covid-19-vaccines/distribution/index.html/
- https://www.csis.org/analysis/global-covid-19-vaccine-distribution-handbook

CHAPTER TWELVE

Indian Foreign Policy and COVID Vaccine

Abstract

India is considered the world's vaccine manufacturing hub. Which contributes 60 percent to the global vaccine supply. The country has the potential to produce three billion coronavirus disease 2019 (Covid-19) vaccine doses annually. India exported Excel to more than 90 countries. Received foreign aid from more than 25 countries. India and other countries around the world continue to fight the covid-19 epidemic. On 19 April 2021, the Press Information Bureau released details of India's immunization strategy. The National Expert Group on Vaccine Administration for Covid-19, chaired by Policy Commission member dr. BK Pal was instrumental in developing the strategy. The first large consignment of millions of doses of the Sputnik 'V vaccine from Russia's Serum Institute and India Biotech is set to arrive in India in May 2021. The second wave of the coronavirus and its tragic consequences have persuaded India to accept foreign aid at intervals of 17 years. It has also had a far-reaching strategic impact on India. As a direct result of the epidemic, India's claim to regional supremacy and leadership could take a big hit. These will affect the content and conduct of India's foreign policy in the years to come.

Keywords: Indian foreign policy, covid-19, covaxin, sputnik v, coronavirus.

Introduction

When the Covid 19 epidemic spread from country to country, from continent to continent. The virus has had a devastating effect on the world economy. There is no doubt that the nations of the first world were not spared from this epidemic. Because the strategic and policy aspects of most countries were unprepared to deal with this serious epidemic crisis. India has not been spared from this epidemic this year. Yet it has partnered with itself in a concerted effort to combat the epidemic. In response to the disaster, the government enacted the Prevention of Epidemic Disease Act of 1897. The Disaster Management Act of 2005 took the advice of medical experts in a less decisive way for policymakers to make the epidemic a national emergency[1]. The epidemic has had a lasting effect on India's foreign policy. The second wave of Covid-19 and its tragic consequences have forced India to accept foreign aid after 17 years. It is bound to have far-reaching strategic implications for India. India's demand for regional supremacy and leadership could be a major blow as a direct result of the epidemic. These will affect the content and conduct of India's foreign policy in the years to come.

The impact of covid-19 on India's foreign policy has led to a decline in India's traditional dominance in the regional arena, material aid, and political influence. The Covid-19 has reduced its ability to help neighbours materially. Because historical ties alone cannot sustain India's regional hegemony. Thought checkbook diplomacy is already pushing India into its strategic location, the Indian subcontinent[2]. The second wave of the Covid-19 accelerated this process. Because India's ability to stand up to China has greatly diminished today. Affects India's involvement with Covid-19. Any ambitious military spending will prevent modernization plans. It will limit the country's focus on global diplomacy and regional geopolitics. With reduced military spending and diplomatic focus on regional geopolitics, India's power will become uncertain.

Who has influenced diplomacy in the Indo-Pacific region:

The effects of Covid-19 have affected economies in the Indo-Pacific region. Unable to play a leading role in the Indo-Pacific project, China has tried to persuade smaller states in the region. And moving forward with the goal of exclusive dominance. Covid-19 is heading for a general economic crisis. As a result, the decline in foreign direct investment and industrial production and rising unemployment are expected to limit India's strategic ambitions. This suggests that Indian foreign policy in the aftermath of Covid-19 may therefore be a holding operation.

Indo-China relations:

Although India and China made a positive start in 2020, the epidemic began to rupture relations immediately. Significant tensions have spread on the border between the two countries. Troops and weapons were completely withdrawn from the north and south shores of Pangong Lake in February, through military and economic talks between India and China since early May 2020. Separate talks are now underway between the fear parties to deal with the remaining clashes. The Indian government banned Chinese products and Chinese apps, especially after the Galloway conflict. At present India-China relations are fragile and it is time to choose between protectionism and full cooperation. It is unknown at this time what he will do after leaving the post[3].

Indo-US relations:

The challenge of the covid epidemic and the change in the US administration have increased the dynamism of the ever-evolving relationship between the two strong democracies. It signed important defence agreements last year. Working towards a formal cut to the Quiet Alliance or actively supporting India during LAC urbanization with China. The Malabar exercise, which took place in November 2020, was a high point in the Indo-US strategic relationship, among the navies of the four quadruple countries. For the first time in three years, a mega naval exercise was held, which sent a strong message to China. However, there have been some ups and downs in Indo-US relations during the epidemic. While the United States was dealing with a deadly covid wave, India helped by providing medical supplies and exports and relaxing export restrictions. However, at the beginning of 2021, when India was going through the same ordeal, the United States was hesitant to show sincerity. The Joe Biden administration's U.S. First Policy the United States quickly changed course and accelerated supplies amid a storm of widespread condemnation around the world. Now is the time when epidemics are still rampant and vaccines are becoming increasingly necessary. Strong Indo-US relations will be important to help prevent global epidemics[4].

The partnership between the United States and India is bound up with a commitment to freedom, democratic principles, equality for all its citizens, and human rights. The United States and India share a common interest in promoting global security, resilience, and economic prosperity through trade investment and similar structures. But during the second wave of the Covid-19 epidemic, there was a delay in US approval of the raw materials needed to make the vaccine in India. At the behest of the public, however, Mohammad Adar Punawala, CO of the Seram Institute of India, played a key role in the outcry against this strong notion, which initially formed the backdrop of Indian foreign policy. However, the United States later revised its position on the issue, and the entire US leadership immediately began sending medical aid to India. They also contacted Indian leader Narendra Modi by phone. Internally, Jute has written realism and is expected to regain its brilliance in the last 4-5 years to show its inclination towards the United States[5]. Indian Foreign Minister Jayashankar, during his visit to New York and Washington, has so far focused on increasing vaccine production and distribution. He called for an agreement at the Security Dialogue Summit in March. Foreign Minister Biden emphasized the need for an intellectual property right over vaccines and other products, such as medical devices and personal protective equipment. The Foreign Minister met with corporate interrogators, including a new global task force, which has further helped raise funds for India.

India-Bangladesh relations:

On March 15, 2020, the Prime Minister of Bangladesh Sheikh Hasina took part in an online video conference with the leaders of SAARC countries at the invitation of Prime Minister Narendra Modi on the current state of the Kovid-19 epidemic. India and Bangladesh have excellent bilateral relations due to their common language, heritage, history, and culture. Since the agenda of the meeting was to stop the spread of the virus, a number of collaborative measures were discussed. 30000 tests including 30000 surgical masks, 15000 headcovers, 50000 surgical gloves, 100000 hydroxychloroquine medicine tablets, and RT-PCR test kits are discussed. In 2021, the Government of India has gifted 2 million covishild vaccines to Bangladesh to help it overcome the epidemic. The Government of Bangladesh has signed a bilateral MOU to procure 30 million doses of covid-19 vaccine from Bangladesh Beximco Pharmaceuticals Limited and the Serum Institute of India[6].

Medical diplomacy:

Historically, India has always been marked by poverty and disease. Even the colonists often painted a picture of an environment full of perpetual plague. Although India has certainly been known since those days. For many years the world has seen the nation not as a provider but as a recipient of global healthcare. However, India's role as an international healthcare provider in the epidemic has changed and its medical diplomacy has moved forward. From hydroxychloroquine medicine to vaccine delivery, India is reaching out to everyone in need. On January 21, 2021, India started promoting its vaccine alliance. Vasudeva Kutumbakam is a family venture inspired by the ancient Indian philosophical doctrine. Oxford AstraZeneca and the Serum Institute of India have provided Covi-shield vaccine, developed in neighbouring Bhutan and the Maldives, in a campaign under Rubric, India's first neighbour policy[7].

India has expanded its presence in South Asia by supplying vaccines to its neighbours Bangladesh, Bhutan, Nepal, Sri Lanka (excluding Pakistan and China) through vaccine alliance initiatives. However, the second wave of pandemic vaccines in India has temporarily suspended the alliance initiative. Trying to increase the impact of thinking about his opportunities. The second wave of the Covid-19 epidemic forced K to accept foreign aid, including the Chinese Red Cross, for the first time in 16 years. The Bhartiya Janata Party-led government of India has to seek foreign aid, which is a shame. This is because seeking help from outside or relying on outsiders is a thundering signal in Indian foreign policy. The call for a virtual conference of South Asian foreign ministers on China's recent vaccine[8] cooperation will have a long-term effect. To free China from its influence in South Asia in the short term, India must first work to earn its credibility internally. For more than two decades, India has earned the reputation of being the "Pharmacy of the World". Because of its strong generic pharmaceutical industry, it has been providing quality medicines at affordable prices in the world market. India has taken steps to reduce the cost of treating affordable AIDS, tuberculosis, and malaria at a time when the Indian company HIV is spreading worldwide. India's generic industry has emerged as the largest supplier. Moreover, the export of medicines from India has indeed increased from 1 1 billion at the beginning of the century to now 20 billion. It plays a historic role as a supplier of affordable medicines. India has taken two significant initiatives to overcome the Covid-19 epidemic. The first is to make vaccines widely available, making the Covid-19 vaccine universally acceptable. Second, the initiative is to submit a joint proposal with South Africa to the WTO, which would provide a temporary exemption from the exercise and exercise of intellectual property rights. The purpose is to try to free the Covid-19 vaccine, medicine, and other medical products from intellectual property rights[9].

On 19 April 2021, the Press Information Bureau released details of India's Covid-19 vaccination strategy, focusing on the scale and speed of the third phase. The National Expert Group on Vaccine Administration for Covid-19, chaired by Dr. V K Pal, a member of the Policy Commission, played a key role in developing the strategy. The first phase of India's Covid-19 mass inflation program was launched on January 16. An estimated 30 million healthcare and frontline workers were covered. On March 1,

Vision launched the second phase, which aimed to cover the illnesses of people over 45 and those over 60. The deadline for vaccinating all people over the age of 45 has been extended to April 1. As a result, over 300 million vaccines have been given. Although only 22 percent of the population[10].

In March 2021, India emerged as one of the leading suppliers of the Covid-19 vaccine. Rainfall has been able to play this role due to its partnership with the Serum Institute of India, the world's largest vaccine manufacturer in terms of dosage. The company claims that it is capable of producing 1.5 billion doses annually. In June 2020, SII signed an agreement with AstraZeneca. It is a British Swedish pharmaceutical company. Oxford University will supply 1 billion doses of the covid vaccine to middle and low-income countries, including India. SII is currently supplying its vaccine "Covi shield" to the Government of India.

How many companies are providing vaccines in India? :

Vaccination is an important part of India's fight against the second Covid-19 wave. Vaccinating about 150 million (850 million) people over the age of 18 is a major challenge for the country. This means that India currently needs 17.7 million vaccines for the entire vaccine. The government has said that India will produce a total of 126 crore vaccines between August and December. The target is to collect more than 35.6 crore doses. However, due to the current inability of India to meet the demand for biotics, the Serum Institute, the world's largest vaccine maker, and Russia's Sputnik 'V Kovid Nineteen Vaccine' have been contracted to arrive in India on 31 May 2021 with the first large consignment of millions. Russia has provided 2 million doses[11].

What is Covaxine ?:

Covaxine is an inactivated vaccine, meaning it is made up of a dead coronavirus. This makes the body safe for injection. Biotic India is a 24-year-old vaccine maker with a portfolio of 16 vaccines and exports to 123 countries. The coronavirus tips isolated by the National Institute of Virology of India used a sample. When administered the immune cells can recognize the still dead virus. The epidemic causes the immune system to produce antibodies against the virus. Two doses are given four weeks apart. The vaccine can be stored at temperatures ranging from 2-degree Celsius to 8 degree Celsius. The effectiveness of the vaccine is 81%. Shows preliminary data from its phase trial. India's regulator gave emergency approval to the vaccine in January. When the third phase of the trial was underway. Experts say India Biotech says it has 20 million doses of vaccine in stock. It aims to produce 700 million doses of its four facilities in the two cities by the end of the year.

What is covidshild ?:

The Oxford AstraZeneca vaccine is being manufactured locally at the Seram Institute of India, the world's largest vaccine manufacturer. It says it made more than 60 million per month. When it is injected into a patient, it triggers the immune system to produce antibodies. Helps to attack any coronavirus infection. The vaccine is given in two doses four to 12 weeks apart. It can be safely stored at temperatures from 2 degrees Celsius to 1 degree Celsius. Doctors can be easily delivered to existing healthcare settings like surgery. The vaccine was developed by Pfizer- Biotech which is currently being operated in several countries. Must be stored at 70 0 C. Only a limited number of jars can be removed. A special challenge in India because summer temperatures there can reach up to 50 degrees Celsius.

What is Sputnik V ?:

The vaccine, developed by the Moscow Camellia Institute, initially sparked some controversy after it rolled out before final test data were released. But scientists say the benefits have now been demonstrated. It uses a cold virus designed to infect the body as a carrier to deliver a small piece of coronavirus. Thus, a part of the genetic defect of the virus can safely expose the body and fight against it without the risk of getting sick. After vaccination, the body begins to produce antibodies to the coronavirus. It can be stored at temperatures up to 8 degrees Celsius from Today Grit which is easy to transport and store.

India's Sputnik V:

According to the report, the Russian direct investment fund, TT Vaccine Marketing, has entered into agreements with six domestic vaccine manufacturers to manufacture 750 million doses of Sputnik V in India. Dr. Reddy's Laboratories, head of pharmaceuticals in Hyderabad, will import the first batch of 125 million doses to India this quarter. The level will be increased in the next quarter when the Indian company starts building under the supervision of Dr. Reddy. Until the day, India will largely rely on the two previously approved candidates, Covacin and Covishield[12].

Government of India and Vaccine Diplomacy:

The Government of India has announced a comprehensive vaccine diplomacy strategy to provide a significant number of vaccines to most of its neighbours and other developing countries, including Africa. India has seven neighbouring countries in South Asia such as Afghanistan,

Bangladesh, Bhutan, Maldives, Nepal, and Sri Lanka. All countries that have already received vaccine assistance are Myanmar and Mauritius. In a South Asian region where China's growing presence has been evident over the years, the Indian government's vaccine diplomacy could play a key role. The real value of India's vaccine diplomacy can be seen in the fact that Canadian Prime Minister Trudeau sought Prime Minister Modi's help in getting the vaccine from SII. But relations between India and Canada have been bitter for months. So, India's vaccine diplomacy has helped normalize.

The Government of India's policy of vaccination with partner countries will undoubtedly serve the welfare of the people of the world. Vaccines and affordable medicine are at the heart of the prospect of a rapid recovery of the global economy from the Cavs 90 crisis. To this end, especially for the citizens of developing countries, India and South Africa took an important initiative to ensure the affordable price of Covid-19 vaccine-related products through their proposal to the WTO in October 2020[13].

Country	Commercial	Supply	Total
Bangladesh	2000	7000	9000
Marocco	0	7000	7000
Brazil	0	4000	4000
Myanmar	1700	2000	3700
Saudi Arabia	0	3000	3000
Nepal	1000	1000	2000
SriLankan	500	500	1000
South Africa	0	1000	1000
Mexico	0	870	870
Ghana	0	600	600
Argentina	0	580	580
Afghanistan	500	0	500
Ukraine	0	500	500
Maldives	200	0	200
Mauritius	100	100	200
Kuwait	0	200	200
United Arab Emirates	0	200	200
Bhutan	150	0	150
Srebia	0	150	150
Magnolia	150	0	150
Bahrain	100	0	100
Oman	100	0	100
Bark dose	100	0	100
UNO	0	100	100
Dominica	70	0	70
Seychelles	50	0	50
Egypt	0	50	50
Algeria	0	50	50
Democratic Republic	30	20	50
L Salvador	0	20	20
Total	6750	28940	35690

Sorce: foreign ministry of India

Conclusion:

In this complex and uncertain time, India's diplomacy has borne fruit in adapting and evolving. All wealth is achieved by growth periods. An economic upsurge occurred after World War II and the Great Depression, and a similar trend was observed after the death of the four greats in the aftermath of World War II. The health crisis has led to significant investments in medicine and public health. The same is expected after the epidemic and India must rise from its responsibility. It is imperative that Kovid-19 goes beyond diplomacy, geopolitics and works for the real welfare of the people in the spirit of Basudev Kutumbakam. In the years to come, India should have a proactive and dynamic global strategy. To emphasize simple alliances and convergence.

Reference:

- Smriti kurup, " impact of covid-19 on India's foreign policy: an analysis", August 6, 2021
- Biswajit Dhar, "India's vaccine diplomacy" April 8, 2021
- Rachit Garg, "Indian foreign policy during the covid-19 pandemic" August 2021
- Rachit Garg, "Indian foreign policy during the covid-19 pandemic" August 2021
- Anuttama Banarjee, " India's flawed vaccine diplomacy", June 25, 2021
- Jabint Jacob,"Indias waxing diplomacy failure and its foreign policy implications", May 19, 2021
- Biswajit Dhar, "India's vaccine diplomacy" April 8, 2021
- Covid-19 vaccines in India, BBC, May 31, 2021
- Covid-19 vaccines in India, BBC, May 31, 2021
- Covid-19 vaccines in India, BBC, May 31, 2021
- Biswajit Dhar, "India's vaccine diplomacy" April 8, 2021

CHAPTER THIRTEEN

Indian Federalism and COVID Vaccines

Abstract

The coronovirus disease , Covid 19, as a pandemic shook the world health care system and economy to such an extent that the epidemic is still spreading and showing no signs of decreasing trend. This pandemic is a dangerous syndrome because it is showing every decade in different forms, such as Severe Acute Respiratory Syndrome (SARS) in 2002, Middle East Respiratory Syndrome (MERS) in 2012 and now Covid 19, Similar epidemics are expected in future also, and this epidemic is changing in unpredictable forms. Thus, the world as such has to face new challenges and issues over time. This article highlights some challenges of containing the coronovirus Covid 19.

Keywords: Covid 19, Vaccination, Challenges, SARS, MERS

Introduction

Federalism is a system of government in which the power is divided between a central authority and various constituent units of the country. A federal government is a system of dividing up power between a central national government and local state governments that are connected to one another by the national government. Some areas of public life are under the control of the national government and some areas are under the control of the local governments. India began the administration of COVID-19 vaccines on 16 January 2021. As of 30 November 2021, India has administered over 1.24 billion doses overall, including first and second doses of the currently-approved vaccines. In India, 80% of the eligible population received at least one shot, and a number of fully vaccinated has surpassed those who have partially jabbed. Coronavirus disease 2019 (COVID19) pandemic, caused by SARS-COV2, is of unprecedented global public health concern. To combat the disease, the Government of India imposed a lockdown in most districts of the 22 States and Union Territories where confirmed cases were reported from March 24, 2020, onwards. The lockdown has been extended till May 31, 2020. The Government of India has claimed success in the fight against the coronavirus pandemic, stating that the number of cases would have been more if the nationwide lockdown had not been imposed. India's response to the COVID-19 pandemic has shifted the balance of its federal structure. The pandemic has enabled the central government to implement far-reaching reforms in areas, such as agriculture, traditionally considered to be the domain of states. This exercise by the central government is indicative of its willingness to take advantage of a global crisis and use the levers of federal power to implement significant reforms. It also indicates that, contrary to conventional wisdom, the constitutional structure of India's federalism is less relevant to the actual relationship between India's national and state governments. The initial stages of the COVID-19 response highlighted the unitary tilt in the Indian federal structure. The central government implemented a national lockdown using its powers under a central disaster management law, and its Ministry of Home Affairs issued extensive guidelines to states for controlling the pandemic. This law empowers the central government to commandeer state and local authorities if necessary. State governments acquiesced even though they have independent powers under a more specific law, the Epidemic Diseases Act, 1897. This arrangement persisted even though the central administration of the lockdown resulted in significant confusion and friction. In fact, state governments requested the central government continue with its administration of the national lockdown during its initial phase. In doing so, states succeed considerable decision-making power and political capital to the central government. Subsequent phases of the lockdown have seen their autonomy restored, but Indian states now have less functional power relative to the center. Since the national lockdown required shutting down almost all economic activity, there was a drastic reduction in revenue for state governments. Even prior to the lockdown, many states in India had already breached or come close to breaching their mandated fiscal deficit limits. The lockdown has further increased their financial dependence on the center. This erosion of political and financial capital has enabled the center to benefit at the expense of states. In May 2020, India's finance minister announced a series of reforms to facilitate India's post-lockdown economic recovery. Many of these measures impinge on the autonomy of state governments and have only been accepted due to the unprecedented situation presented by the pandemic.

Objectives of the Study

- To discuss the Indian Federal System during the period of COVID-19.
- To discuss the initiatives taken by the Indian government during the COVID period towards its States and UTs.
- To discuss how the Indian Government help States to provide COVID vaccine to different States.

India's Battle with COVID-19

Many countries have been through multiple waves of the pandemic since the first cases were reported in December 2019 from Wuhan China. After the first case, reported on 30th January 2020, the governments at various levels took precautionary measures: thermal screening of passengers at airports; cancellation of international flights from affected countries and banning mass congregations. A number of states also imposed partial lockdowns and sealed their borders. On 24th March 2020, the central government announced a three-week-long nationwide lockdown. The central government would later extend the lockdown until 1st may 2020 as many states had demanded, it would again be stretched up to 17th May, although with certain relaxations from 18th May, the central government in consultation with the states began the unlocking process in various phases until October. The crisis overwhelmed a number of states, such as Maharashtra, Gujarat, Tamil Nadu, and Delhi. India managed to contain the first wave with a combination of strict lockdowns, the rapid expansion of healthcare infrastructure, and effective coordination between the center and state government. By early March, India saw the onslaught of the second wave. A new variant accelerated the pace of infections in many states including Maharashtra, Gujarat, Punjab and Delhi. The cases would engulf most regions by the end of April with states such as Maharashtra, Uttar Pradesh, Karnataka, Goa, Gujarat, Haryana and metro cities like Delhi and Bangalore getting completely overwhelmed by the exponential surge in infections. Images of people desperately looking for medical oxygen, medicines and hospital beds on their own, made headlines across the globe. By June, India had recorded as many as 29, 700, 313 cases and 381, 931 deaths, second only to the United States.

In terms of response, the second wave did not witness a national lockdown or strictly enforced central guidelines from the ministry of Home Affairs. The center has largely left the decision-making to the state governments. As a result, states announced localized lockdowns in April and May have followed pandemic guidelines or protocols based on their needs. Testing in the early days of the pandemic was limited to a few public laboratories. Private laboratories, which typically provide the bulk of pathology services, were not allowed to test at all. Testing rates have been highly variable across states. Daily testing in Delhi, the capital city was around 670 per million at the end of July comparable to that in the United States but rates elsewhere were much lower. As an August 4th, the state of Bihar was conducting just 20,000 tests per day, for a population of 105 million.

Center's distribution of COVID-19 vaccines among States or UTs

Allocation of COVID-19 vaccines to a State is done based on its population, caseload, utilization efficiency and wastage factors, the Union Health Ministry said. The Ministry said the allegations of non-transparent distribution of vaccines among States are "completely without any basis, and not fully informed". It clarified that the Government of India continues to allocate COVID-19 vaccines to States and Union Territories in a transparent manner based on the population of a State, its caseload, its utilization efficiency and wastage factors. In a statement, the Ministry said India's COVID vaccination programme is built on scientific and epidemiological evidence, WHO guidelines and global best practices. Anchored in systematic end-to-end planning, it is implemented through effective and efficient participation of States and Union Territories and the public. Information about the vaccine supply by the Government of India, consumption by the States and Union Territories, vaccine doses available with them, along vaccine supply in the pipeline is regularly shared through press releases by the Press Information Bureau, and also through other forums, the statement said. But we will see in table that it did not cover up the whole population of India. Many of states got very less percentage of doses as according to their population.

Vaccination rollout Statistics by State or UTs

State/union territory	Population (2011 census)	1st dose	2nd dose	Cumulative doses administered	Percentage of people given one dose	Percentage of people fully vaccinated
	[illegible]	[illegible]	[illegible]	[illegible]	[illegible]	[illegible]
Andaman and Nicobar Islands	[illegible]	[illegible]	[illegible]	[illegible]	[illegible]	[illegible]
Andhra Pradesh	[illegible]	[illegible]	[illegible]	[illegible]	[illegible]	[illegible]
Arunachal Pradesh	[illegible]	[illegible]	[illegible]	[illegible]	[illegible]	[illegible]
Assam	[illegible]	[illegible]	[illegible]	[illegible]	[illegible]	[illegible]
Bihar	[illegible]	[illegible]	[illegible]	[illegible]	[illegible]	[illegible]
Chandigarh	[illegible]	[illegible]	[illegible]	[illegible]	[illegible]	[illegible]
Chhattisgarh	[illegible]	[illegible]	[illegible]	[illegible]	[illegible]	[illegible]
Dadra and Nagar Haveli and Daman and Diu	[illegible]	[illegible]	[illegible]	[illegible]	[illegible]	[illegible]
Delhi	[illegible]	[illegible]	[illegible]	[illegible]	[illegible]	[illegible]
Goa	[illegible]	[illegible]	[illegible]	[illegible]	[illegible]	[illegible]
Gujarat	[illegible]	[illegible]	[illegible]	[illegible]	[illegible]	[illegible]
Haryana	[illegible]	[illegible]	[illegible]	[illegible]	[illegible]	[illegible]
Himachal Pradesh	[illegible]	[illegible]	[illegible]	[illegible]	[illegible]	[illegible]
Jammu and Kashmir	[illegible]	[illegible]	[illegible]	[illegible]	[illegible]	[illegible]
Jharkhand	[illegible]	[illegible]	[illegible]	[illegible]	[illegible]	[illegible]
Karnataka	[illegible]	[illegible]	[illegible]	[illegible]	[illegible]	[illegible]
Kerala	3,34,06,061	2,43,41,295	1,03,31,760	3,46,73,055	73%	31%

State/union territory	Population (2011 census)	1st dose	2nd dose	Cumulative doses administered	Percentage of people given one dose	Percentage of people fully vaccinated
	[illegible]	[illegible]	[illegible]	[illegible]	[illegible]	[illegible]
Ladakh	2,74,000	2,02,848	1,32,008	3,34,856	74%	48%
Lakshadweep	64,473	54,576	39,315	93,891	85%	61%
Madhya Pradesh	7,26,26,809	4,63,62,905	1,35,18,828	5,98,81,731	64%	19%
Maharashtra	11,23,74,333	5,48,12,576	2,21,08,614	7,69,21,190	49%	20%
Manipur	25,70,390	12,17,411	4,34,132	16,51,543	47%	17%
Meghalaya	29,66,889	10,63,908	4,31,973	14,95,881	36%	15%
Miscellaneous	—	19,02,795	15,58,835	34,61,630	—	—
Mizoram	10,97,206	6,90,706	4,02,479	10,93,185	63%	37%
Nagaland	19,78,502	6,79,956	3,26,310	10,06,266	34%	16%
Odisha	4,19,74,219	2,12,72,105	78,32,873	2,91,04,978	51%	19%
Puducherry	12,47,953	6,82,803	2,77,135	9,59,938	55%	22%
Punjab	2,77,43,338	1,38,76,483	46,32,092	1,85,08,575	50%	17%
Rajasthan	6,85,48,437	3,95,44,905	1,45,12,093	5,40,56,998	58%	21%
Sikkim	6,10,577	5,16,318	3,51,985	8,68,303	85%	58%

State/union territory	Population (2011 census)	1st dose	2nd dose	Cumulative doses administered	Percentage of people given one dose	Percentage of people fully vaccinated
	121.0 crore	[illegible]	[illegible]	[illegible]	[illegible]	[illegible]
Tamil Nadu	7,21,47,030	3,41,18,725	95,80,398	4,36,99,126	47%	13%
Telangana	3,50,03,674	1,71,85,597	64,43,755	2,36,29,352	49%	18%
Tripura	36,73,917	24,89,252	12,71,721	37,60,973	68%	35%
Uttar Pradesh	19,98,12,341	8,08,85,097	1,79,98,110	9,88,83,207	40%	9%
Uttarakhand	1,00,86,292	72,94,328	29,23,712	1,02,18,040	72%	29%
West Bengal	9,12,76,115	3,84,07,873	1,56,35,624	5,40,43,497	42%	17%
As of October 14, 2021 7:00 AM IST						

Global distribution of COVID Vaccine by India

India plays a very important role to distribute COVID vaccines at the global level also. In January 2021, India began a humanitarian initiative known as Vaccine Maitri (vaccine friendship), which aims to leverage the country's pharmaceutical industry to export Indian-manufactured vaccines to other countries. The Ministry of External Affairs stated that since 20 January, India had donated over 5.5 million vaccines to neighboring countries such as Bahrain, Bangladesh, Bhutan, Maldives, Mauritius, Myanmar, Nepal, Seychelles, and Sri Lanka and that the country was also planning to send doses to Africa, Nicaragua, Oman, the Caribbean Community, and the COVAX programme, and to distribute vaccines to other countries via commercial exports. The Ministry of External Affairs stated that "In line with the Prime Minister's announcement that India sees international cooperation in the fight against the COVID-19 pandemic as its duty, we have played the role of the first responder in our neighborhood as well as undertaken supplies to countries beyond." In response to these donations, Secretary-General of the United Nations Antonio Guterres stated that he "strongly hope that India will have all the instruments that are necessary to play a major role in making sure that a global vaccination is campaign is made possible", and went on to say that, "I think that the production capacity of India is the best asset that the world has today. I hope the world understands that it must be fully used". As of 10 March

2021, India had distributed over 58 million vaccine doses to 65 nations through the scheme, but due to India's domestic need for vaccines, these exports were suspended later in March and the suspension was expected to continue throughout 2021. The Health Minister of India, Mr. Mansukh Mandaviya announced in September that India will resume the export of vaccines from October to the rest of the world.

The Way Forward

India is a large country, and it does not face a single homogenous epidemic. Currently, 80% of cases are reported from more than10% of its districts. The epidemic is in different stages in different parts of the country, but the response has been driven by a national, overarching centralized strategy instead of being locally owned. Although opportunities for containment of infections are limited, given the tremendous economic and human cost of lockdowns, a number of measures could help reduce the mortality rate and facilitate a quicker exit from the pandemic.

- An important aspect of COVID-19 management is averting deaths. The current national guidelines do not prioritize high-risk individuals for early testing, and this is a missed opportunity for averting deaths in vulnerable populations of the elderly and those with comorbidities.
- Reporting of deaths is incomplete, and because many individuals die without a COVID-19 test, the number of reported deaths is likely an underestimate of the true numbers. Identification of deaths offers an opportunity to learn about the disease and, thereby, prevent future cases and deaths. A formal system of mortality surveillance, specifically to measure the additional mortality attributable to COVID-19, needs to be put in place.[19]
- The epidemic response should be data-driven and locally owned. More granular data and greater openness to data sharing and coordination would enable surveillance data to be used for management decisions, including planning regarding personal protective equipment, medicines, supplies, and, most importantly, ICU capacity and healthcare personnel. This would provide a clear picture of the impact of COVID-19 to the public and could encourage greater compliance with personal protection and distancing.
- Nongovernmental organizations and civil society have been largely missing from the response to the pandemic and should be involved in helping mitigate the continued effects of the lockdown and enabling

access to health care.

- Guidelines for clinical protocols for patient management should be updated rapidly, consistent with global research findings, and communicated clearly to clinicians. Despite national guidelines, there is confusion about how best to care for patients at home with asymptomatic infection, in hospitals with mild-to-moderate disease, with a serious disease requiring high flow oxygen, and with severe disease requiring mechanical ventilation.

The COVID-19 pandemic is an opportunity to invest in the public health infrastructure of India, an area of systemic neglect over the past few decades. In the short-to-medium term, developing protocols for clinical trials to investigate candidate vaccines, drugs, and monoclonal antibodies against SARS-CoV-2 infection will be critical to ensure optimal preventive and therapeutic management of the disease, particularly to protect those at high risk of death.[21] In the long term, a blueprint should be developed to empower and strengthen India's national and state-level mechanisms for public health research, surveillance, and policy activities. As was the case in other countries, India's pandemic preparedness plan was largely abandoned in the face of a real pandemic. The response to COVID-19 has been driven by political priorities rather than by public health and epidemiological expertise.

Given the country's size and its large global Diaspora, India's battle with COVID-19 will play a large role in the fate of the pandemic. As the world's largest vaccine producer, India will likely be a major supplier of vaccines against COVID-19, if and when they are approved. The country's largest vaccine manufacturers are gearing up to produce COVID-19 vaccines at scales that have not been attempted before. If India's vaccine industry is successful, then it will help ensure that these vaccines will be available not only to those who can pay for them but also to the hundreds of millions of impoverished people in India and in other low- and middle-income countries who need a vaccine. India stands at a critical juncture. Although COVID-19 is exacting a significant health and economic impact on the country, it offers an opportunity to rethink India's approach to public health. If done correctly, the legacy of COVID-19 could be a much needed public investment in health, a well-equipped workforce to respond to future pandemics, and system capacity for surveillance, contact tracing, research, disease modeling, and response.

Conclusion

Constitutional provisions and existing legislations confer the primary responsibility for handling a situation like the COVID-19 pandemic, to the state government. Nonetheless, the Centre assumed the role of anchor and led from the front in managing the pandemic, particularly during the periods involving national lockdowns (24 March – 31 May 2020). As the pandemic threatened human lives and livelihoods, demanding swift action on a national scale, the Centre took over the many responsibilities which otherwise fall within the domain of the state. Among many comprehensive measures, the Centre took a series of decisions to scale up vaccine procurement, knowledge production for setting standards and guidelines for the state and local governments, and mitigation of inter-state externalities. Moreover, the Centre's blanket decisions and stringent measures regarding lockdowns and containment zoning—implemented without adequate knowledge of the ground situation-impeded the states' capacity to combat the spread of the virus. For instance, the states were not allowed to purchase medical kits on their own without the Centre's permission. This impacted the states' ability to mobilize and augment critical resources. In several instances, the MHA deputed supervisory teams to states to monitor their responses to the pandemic without consulting the respective state governments. Therefore, the pandemic brought the wider powers of the Centre in full display, especially during the early phase: it was the Centre that imposed the lockdown, and it was also the Centre that monitored state responses including physical-distancing norms, regulation of economic activities, and provision of financial packages. The most fundamental lesson from India's experience with the second wave of the COVID-19 pandemic is that managing a grave national crisis requires healthy cooperation between the Centre and states. The federal government must be prepared to take the anchor's role.

References

- Amrita Madhukalya(2020), "Covid-19: States protest against Centre's directive on PPE procurement", *Hindustan times*
- Anirudh Burman(2020), "How Covid-19 is changing Indian federalism", Carnegie India
- Anshu Sharma et.al (2020), "Lockdown relaxation: States to decide, but within Home Ministry guidelines", *CNBC TV*

- Alain G. Gagnon et.al (2001), *Multinational Democracy*, Cambridge University Press
- Edwin T. Why migrant workers are protesting: No money to buy essentials, limited access to cooked food. https://www.thehindubusinessline.com/news/why-migrant-workers-are-protesting-no-money-to-buy-essentials-limited-access-to-cooked-food/article31352912.ece
- Gupta A, (2020). Tracking COVID-19 mortality in India, where deaths aren't registered properly. *The Wire Science*. Available at: https://science.thewire.in/health/covid-19-mortality-india-civil-registration-deaths/.

- Guermond .V.et.al (2020), How coronavirus could hit the billions migrant workers send home.*World Economic Forum*
- https://www.thehindu.com/news/national/distribution-of-covid-19-vaccines-among-states-done-in-transparent-manner-centre/article34958808.ece
- Hodgson J, (2020), the pandemic pipeline. *Nat Biotechnology* 38: 523–532
- *International Journal of Infectious disease* vol.104, March 2021
- Karmis, Dimitrios et.al (2005), *Theories of Federalism: A Reader*, New York
- Lorenz C, Azevedo et.al (2020), COVID-19 and dengue fever: a dangerous combination for the health system in Brazil. *Travel Med Infect Dis* 35: 101659.
- Mishra H.H. Coronavirus lockdown: *how to keep 130 million migrant workers afloat during COVID-19 crisis.*
- Niranjan Sahoo(2020), "Covid-19 and Cooperative federalism in India: So Far, so good", *ORF Expert Speak*
- Press Trust of India W. Remittances to India likely to decline by 23% in 2020 due to covid-19: World Bank.
- Sharma N.C (2020), Private Hospitals stare at losses amid covid outbreak. Livemint.
- Srinivas Chokkakula,(2020) "India's response to Covid-19 reflects the power, problems, potential of federalism", *The Indian Express*
- The Indian Council of Medical Research (ICMR), 2020. *ICMR Press Statement*. Available at: https://www.icmr.gov.in/media.html

CHAPTER FOURTEEN

Natural immunity versus vaccination immunity

Introduction

The presence of antibodies to a disease in a person's system confers immunity to that disease. Antibodies are proteins that the body produces to neutralise or destroy toxins or disease-carrying organisms. Antibodies have a disease-specific function. Measles antibody, for example, will protect a person if he or she is exposed to measles disease but will have no effect if he or she is exposed to mumps.

The immune system has two parts:

- Innate (non-specific) immune response
- Acquired (specific) immune response

The non-specific innate immune response is the body's initial response to external threats. Immune cells detect a possible threat and raise the alarm, triggering the inflammatory response.

The acquired immune response is a targeted defence against external invaders. T cells, B cells, and antibodies are key actors in the acquired immune response:

T cells are immunological cells with a variety of functions. As part of the antibody manufacturing process, helper T cells interact with B cells and activate cytotoxic T cells to attack the pathogen.

B cells are immune cells that travel throughout the body, interact with antigen-presenting cells, activate helper T cells, convert into plasma B cells, and generate large amounts of antibodies.

Antibodiesare proteins produced by B cells that are intended to identify a specific foreign material known as an antigen.

Immunological Memory

Immunological memory is the ability of the immune system to retain information about a specific pathogen in preparation for future attacks by that pathogen. T cells, B cells, and antibodies all play a role in this process.

Immunological memory is a key concept in vaccine development because vaccines function by inducing an early immune response that establishes immunological memory without causing illness. As a result, when a person comes into contact with a "real" infection, his or her immune system is already prepared with the necessary machinery to protect the body[1].

The innate immune system completes the body's first reaction to SARS-CoV-2, followed by the adaptive immune system. Innate immune cells identify the viral particle and eliminate it while also communicating to other cells.

As a result of this signalling, the host develops protection to limit viral transmission from the infected cell to other cells nearby. In many cases, especially in moderate or asymptomatic infection, the innate immune response appears to be adequate to completely eradicate the virus.

T-cells are then recruited to kill infected cells as a result of this occurrence. Only when T-cells identify antigens presented by MHC class I and II molecules can this be accomplished.

The antibody immunoglobulin M (IgM) response develops at the same period. IgM is a multivalent antibody that plays an important role in immunological regulation during the early stages of infection. Memory B-cells, both unswitched IgM+ and classical switched cells, are produced at this stage and can last for months[2].

people with acquired immunity may have differing levels of protection to emerging SARS-CoV-2 variants. More importantly, the data provide further documentation that those who've had and recovered from a COVID-19 infection still stand to benefit from getting vaccinated.

SARS-outer CoV-2's surface is studded with the receptor binding domain (RBD), a critical component of the spike protein. This RBD is particularly essential because the virus uses this portion of its spike protein to bind to ACE2 on human cells before infecting them. As a result, RBD is a primary target for both naturally occurring and vaccine-induced antibodies.

A prior research by the Seattle group used a technique called deep mutational scanning to map out all conceivable changes in the RBD that might affect the virus's capacity to bind ACE2 and/or the ability of RBDdirected antibodies to hit their targets[3].

Natural acquired immunity

Natural infection confers greater protection than vaccine-acquired immunity for several infectious illnesses for which vaccines are available. “Immunity from illness generally follows a single natural infection [but] immunity from vaccinations normally emerges only after multiple doses,” according to the Children’s Hospital of Philadelphia (CHOP). When it comes to chickenpox, you’re generally immune after only one episode, but people require two doses of the vaccine to achieve efficient and long-lasting protection.

People generally become unwell as a result of germ interactions unless they are exposed to a substantial number of virus or bacteria, which is one of the reasons natural immunity is so strong. To this large "dose" of germs, the immune system generates a robust reaction. Many of the unpleasant symptoms you experience while you’re unwell, such as tiredness, fever, and chills, are caused by this strong reaction.

Numerous pathogens, such as the human papillomavirus (HPV), have evolved to avoid detection by the immune system. In 90% of instances, a healthy immune system clears HPV, but those who are immunosuppressed are more prone to long-term infection and reinfection.

The most significant disadvantage of spontaneous infection is that there is no way of knowing how bad the illness will be in advance. Chickenpox is a bothersome illness for the majority of individuals. However, some patients suffer a lung infection, a brain bulge, or a life-threatening blood infection. Prior to the widespread availability of chickenpox vaccines, around 10,000 individuals in the United States were hospitalised each year due to chickenpox complications, and approximately 100 people died from chickenpox each year.

Vaccine-acquired immunity

Vaccines increase the production of antibodies and memory cells in the body, which are needed to combat particular illnesses. The chickenpox vaccine includes very small quantities of weakened (attenuated) chickenpox virus, just enough to get the immune system producing antibodies but not enough to produce chickenpox blisters.

The polio and influenza vaccinations include inactivated (or "killed") viruses, which cannot cause disease but do stimulate the immune system. COVID-19 mRNA vaccines educate cells how to manufacture spike proteins similar to those seen on coronaviruses, which the body then builds antibodies against.

Although side effects like pain and fever are typical after immunisation, most individuals don't feel nearly as bad as they do after contracting an illness.

In some cases, vaccine-acquired immunity is stronger than natural immunity. According to CHOP, HPV, tetanus, *Haemophilus influenzae* type b (Hib), and pneumococcal vaccines induce a better immune response than natural infection [4].

Natural vs. vaccine immunity for COVID-19

For COVID-19, researchers are currently learning about natural and vaccine-induced immunity. Both COVID-19 infection and COVID-19 vaccination, according to healthcare experts, induce immunity that lasts at least eight months. This protection isn't total; it's possible to develop COVID-19 after receiving the vaccine or contracting the virus before, though these cases are seldom serious.

COVID-19 immunisation after infection may "sharpen immunity," according to some data. According to numerous studies, vaccination following COVID-19 recovery boosts antibody production and lowers the risk of reinfection[4].

Vaccines: How Do Work?

Germs may be found in our surroundings as well as in our bodies. When a vulnerable individual comes into contact with a dangerous microbe, it can result in sickness and death.

The human body contains a variety of defence mechanisms against infections (disease-causing organisms). Skin, mucus, and cilia (microscopic hairs that sweep waste away from the lungs) all function as physical barriers to keep infections out of the body.

When a pathogen infects our bodies, our bodies' defences, known as the immune system, are activated, and the infection is fought, killed, or overcome.

The human body's natural response

A pathogen is a bacteria, virus, parasite, or fungus that may infect the body and cause disease. Each infection has many subunits that are generally distinct to that pathogen and the sickness it produces. An antigen is a component of a pathogen that induces the production of antibodies.

The immune system relies heavily on antibodies generated in reaction to the pathogen's antigen. Antibodies can be thought of as troops in your body's defensive mechanism. Our system's antibodies, or soldiers, have been taught to detect a single antigen. Our bodies contain hundreds of different antibodies. When the human body is initially exposed to an antigen, it takes time for the immune system to react and create antigen-specific antibodies.

Meanwhile, the individual is at risk of falling unwell.

Antigen-specific antibodies are generated and cooperate with the rest of the immune system to kill the infection and stop the illness from spreading. Antibodies to one disease seldom protect against antibodies to another pathogen, unless the two infections are highly related, such as relatives. When the body generates antibodies in response to an antigen, it also develops antibody-producing memory cells, which linger on even after the pathogen has been destroyed by the antibodies. When the body is exposed to the same pathogen several times, the antibody response is considerably quicker and more efficient than it is the first time.

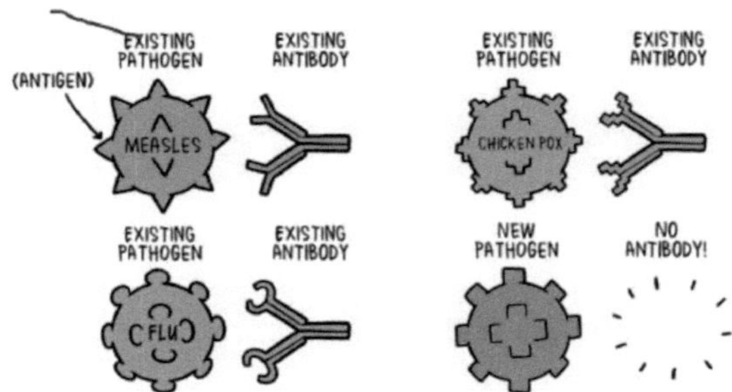

When a new pathogen or disease enters our body, it introduces a new antigen. For every new antigen, our body needs to build a specific antibody that can grab onto the antigen and defeat the pathogen.

How Vaccines Work

Vaccines include weakened or inactive bits of a certain organism (antigen) that cause the body to respond with an immune response. Rather of the antigen itself, newer vaccinations contain the blueprint for manufacturing antigens. This weakened version will not cause disease in the person receiving the vaccine, regardless of whether the vaccine is made up of the antigen itself or the blueprint for the body to produce the antigen, but it will prompt their immune system to respond much like it would on its first reaction to the actual pathogen.

Herd immunity

Some vaccinations require many doses separated by weeks or months. This is sometimes required to allow for the formation of memory cells and the generation of long-lasting antibodies. In this approach, the body is taught to resist a specific disease-causing organism, and the pathogen's memory is built up so that it may be quickly combated if and when it is exposed in the future.

When someone is vaccinated, they are almost certainly protected against the illness being targeted. However, not everyone is fit for vaccination. Certain vaccinations may not be available to people who have underlying health problems that impair their immune systems (such as cancer or HIV) or who have severe sensitivities to specific vaccine components. These individuals can still be protected if they live in an environment where others have been vaccinated. When a large number of people in a community are vaccinated, the disease has a difficult time spreading since the majority of the people it comes into contact with are immune. As a result, the more individuals who are vaccinated, the less probable it is that those who are immune to vaccinations would contract ebola.

This is especially essential for individuals who are not only unable to receive vaccinations but may also be more susceptible to the diseases against which we vaccinate. There is no one vaccine that gives 100 percent protection, and herd immunity does not protect people who cannot be immunised properly. However, because individuals around them have been vaccinated, these people will have significant protection owing to herd immunity.

Vaccination protects not only you, but also people in your community who are unable to receive vaccinations. Vaccinate yourself if you are able.

A vaccine protects an individual...

later, as part of the real organism, it already knows how to defeat it.

A vaccine protects an individual...

Community vaccination protects the whole community, even those who can't vaccinate.

later, as part of the real organism, it already knows how to defeat it.

Humans have produced vaccinations for a variety of life-threatening illnesses throughout history, including meningitis, tetanus, measles, and wild poliovirus.[5]

Outcome of Research about natural immunity vs. acquired immunity

Natural immunity is riskier than acquired immunity. The chance of acquiring a major vaccine-related adverse effect is substantially lower than the risk of serious consequences if infected for all vaccine-preventable diseases. COVID-19 infection can lead to hospitalisation and long-term adverse effects, such as post-COVID-19 syndrome (also known as "long-haul COVID"). Although there are recognised risk factors for severe COVID-19, such as heart disease, thousands of people have developed severe COVID-19 despite having none of these risk factors. A COVID-19 vaccination recipient is unlikely to need hospitalisation or suffer post-COVID-19 syndrome[4].

COVID-19 vaccinations are still considered to be safe and effective. They keep people from becoming sick, going to the hospital, and dying. Furthermore, even in rare occurrences of COVID-19, persons who have been fully or partially vaccinated are more likely to have a milder and shorter illness than those who have not been vaccinated. The Centers for Disease Control and Prevention (CDC) continues to recommend that everyone aged 12 and above get vaccinated against COVID-19 [6].

Reference

- https://wholisticmatters.com/immune-system-support-stress-management/
- https://www.news-medical.net/news/20210810/Natural-vs-vaccine-induced-COVID-19-immunity.aspx
- https://directorsblog.nih.gov/2021/06/22/.
- https://www.healthgrades.com/right-care/vaccines
- https://www.who.int/news-room/feature-stories/detail
- https://www.cdc.gov/media/releases/2021/s0806-vaccination-protection.html

CHAPTER FIFTEEN

COVID vaccines: A step toward averting the pandemic

Abstract

Covid-19 vaccines were created utilising research that has been around for quite some time. There hasn't been any testing done on these vaccinations. In the hopes of producing a new breakthrough, they've gone through every stage of scientific study and development. Furthermore, various health organisations are regularly monitoring particular Covid-19 vaccinations due to the massive devastation caused by the Covid-19 virus. As a result, it is critical that everyone participates in vaccination programmes sponsored by their local government and other organisations on a regular basis. To ensure you don't miss out on the Covid-19 vaccine, here's a summary of key immunisation information.

Covid-19 vaccines have been studied by a number of drug regulatory bodies across the world. They've been demonstrated to help reduce your risks of contracting COVID-19. Your body will be better prepared to defend against additional illnesses once you've been vaccinated if your immune system has been strengthened.

Introduction

Effectivesss of Vaccines against Covid-19

Vaccines against Covid-19 have been evaluated by a number of drug regulatory agencies across the world. They have been shown to be useful in lowering your chances of getting COVID-19.

By being vaccinated, you are helping to improve public health. When you get vaccinated, your body is better prepared to defend against more illnesses because your immune system is strengthened. At the same time, you are defending yourself and the people around you.

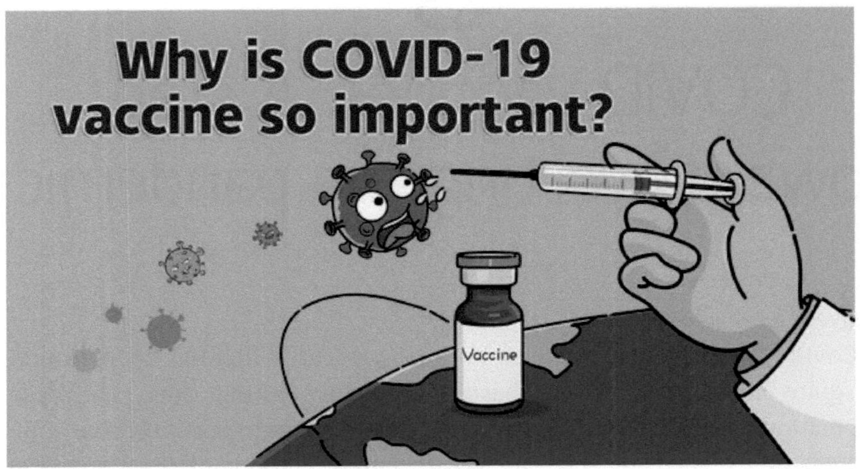

Source: news.cgtn.com

Vaccinations are proven to improve your immune system by training your body how to resist dangers, making them a safe approach to developing your immune system. As a result, many people think of vaccines as a means to strengthen your immune system and the way your body reacts to external objects.

There is no Covid. Vaccines can infect you with Covid: Many people mistakenly assume that because the vaccination contains a strand of the virus, you will get infected. Because a virus does not damage the body in this way, being sick with the vaccination illness poses no risk to you.

Multiple organizations have certified Covid Vaccines.

Several certification authorities have certified the Covid Vaccines that are offered to societies, governments, and other people-bodies, and they have all met incredibly stringent success standards. If a vaccine is certified, you may be confident that it has been thoroughly tested. There are no legitimate reasons for anyone to refuse a Covid-19 vaccination, and it is our responsibility at Pathkind laboratories to allay any fears they may have. There are no compelling reasons to forego the covid-19 vaccine, but there are plenty of compelling ones to do so. Pathkind laboratories test for Covid-19, as well as a range of other diseases, disorders, and infections. When it comes to health tests and analyses, our team of professionals has gained knowledge from years of experience and is your first option.

High COVID-19 vaccination rates were projected to lower SARS-CoV-2 transmission in communities by reducing the number of probable transmission sources and, as a result, the COVID-19 disease burden. Recent results, on the other hand, suggest that the epidemiological significance of COVID-19 vaccine recipients is growing. Secondary attack rates among household contacts exposed to fully vaccinated index cases were identical to secondary attack rates among household contacts exposed to unvaccinated index cases in the United Kingdom (25 percent for vaccinated vs. 23 percent for unvaccinated).

Fully vaccinated index cases were responsible for 12 of the 31 infections in fully vaccinated home contacts (39 percent). Peak viral load was unaffected by vaccination status or variant type.

The incidence of symptomatic COVID-19 cases among fully vaccinated persons ("breakthrough infections") has been monitored weekly in Germany since July 21, 2021, and at the time, it was 16.9% among patients aged 60 and higher.

This percentage is rising week by week, reaching 58.9% on October 27, 2021.

(Figure 1), demonstrating the growing importance of fully vaccinated people as a prospective source of transmission.

A comparable situation exists in the United Kingdom. Between weeks 39 and 42, a total of 100.160 COVID-19 cases were reported among those aged 60 and higher. There were 89.821 cases among the fully vaccinated (89.7%), and 3.395 cases among the unvaccinated (3.4%). [In all age groups of 30 years or more, the COVID-19 case rate per 100.000 was higher in the vaccinated sample compared to the unvaccinated subgroup one week previously. In Israel, a nosocomial outbreak involving 16 healthcare workers, 23 patients, and two family members was recorded. The source was a COVID-19 patient who had been fully immunised. 96.2 percent of those who were exposed to the virus were immunised (151 healthcare workers and 97 patients). Two people who were not protected developed a mild sickness, but fourteen people who had been fully vaccinated became very ill or died.

The US Centers for Disease Control and Prevention classifies four of the top five counties with the highest proportion of completely vaccinated persons (99.9–84.3%) as "high" transmission counties (CDC). [Many decisionmakers consider that immunised people are unlikely to constitute a transmission source.] It appears to be unnecessarily reckless to ignore the vaccinated population as a valid and significant source of transmission when deciding on public health management strategies.

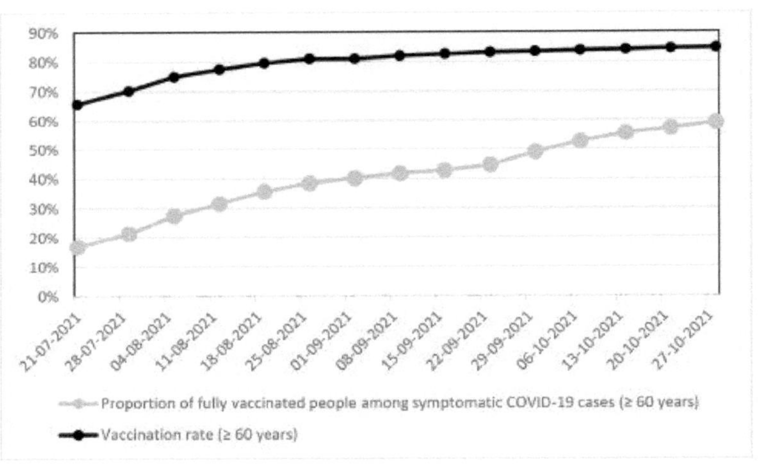

Between July 21 and July 27, vaccination rates and proportions of completely vaccinated people among symptomatic COVID-19 patients (60 years) in Germany were shown.

A COVID-19 epidemic is sweeping the globe. WHO and partners are scrambling to develop and deploy safe and effective vaccinations while they work together on the response — tracking the epidemic, advising on essential measures, and sending important medical supplies to individuals in need.

Every year, vaccines save millions of lives. Vaccines function by teaching and preparing the body's natural defenses, the immune system, to detect and combat the viruses and bacteria they are designed to combat. If the body is later exposed to such disease-causing microorganisms after vaccination, the body is ready to kill them right away preventing sickness.

Source: mayoclinic.org

COVID-19 vaccinations are safe and effective in preventing individuals from becoming very sick or dying. In addition to remaining at least 1 meter away from people, hiding a cough or sneeze in your elbow, constantly wiping your hands, wearing a mask, and avoiding poorly ventilated rooms or opening a window, this is one element of treating COVID-19.

WHO has determined that the following vaccines against COVID-19 have satisfied the relevant safety and effectiveness requirements as of November 15, 2021:

- AstraZeneca/Oxford vaccine
- Johnson and Johnson
- Moderna
- Pfizer/BioNTech

- Sinopharm
- Sinovac
- COVAXIN

Other COVID-19 vaccine preparations have also been evaluated for use in some countries by national regulators.

Even if you've previously had COVID-19, take whatever vaccination is made available to you first. It is critical to be vaccinated as soon as possible as your turn comes up. Although no vaccination is 100 percent protective, approved COVID-19 vaccines offer a high level of protection against becoming extremely sick and dying from the illness.

Which People Should Be Vaccinated?

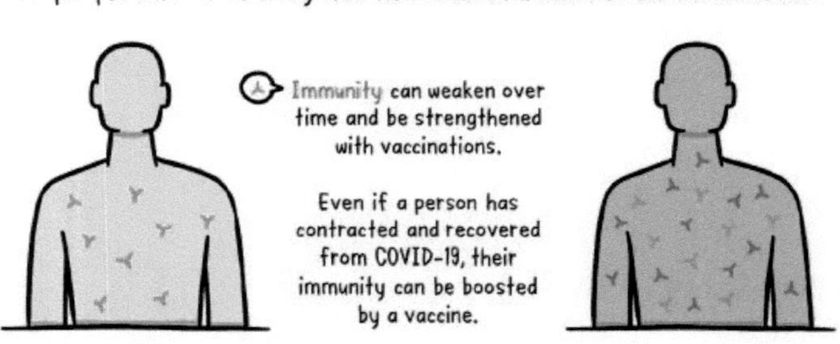

Source: who.int

Most persons aged 18 and above, including those with pre-existing diseases of any type, including auto-immune disorders, are safe to receive the COVID-19 immunizations. Hypertension, diabetes, asthma, lung, liver, and renal illness, as well as stable and well-controlled chronic infections, are among these ailments.

If supplies are limited in your region, talk to your doctor if you have a damaged immune system, are pregnant, or have a history of serious allergies, particularly to vaccines (or any of the ingredients in the vaccine)

- **Have a fragile constitution.**

Because children and adolescents have milder illnesses than adults, they require fewer vaccinations than older people, individuals with chronic health problems, and health professionals, unless they belong to a group at higher risk of serious COVID-19 infection.

More research on the use of the different COVID-19 vaccines in children is needed before general recommendations on vaccinating children against COVID-19 can be made.

Pfizer/BioNTech vaccine is safe for everyone aged 12 and up, according to the WHO's Strategic Advisory Group of Experts (SAGE). Children aged 12 to 15 who are at high risk, as well as other priority groups for vaccination, may get this vaccine. Vaccine trials for children are now underway, and the WHO will revise its recommendations if new evidence or the epidemiological situation becomes available.The recommended childhood vaccines must be received by all children.

What Should I Do After I've Been Vaccinated, And What Can I Expect?

If you experience an unexpected reaction, stay at the vaccination site for at least 15 minutes thereafter so that medical experts can help you.

If you need a second dose, check with your doctor to see when you should return. The majority of vaccines are given in two doses. Consult your doctor to see if a second dose is necessary and when you should take it. Second doses help to strengthen immunity and the immune system's reaction.

In most cases, minor side effects are common. Following immunisation, the following are frequent adverse effects that indicate a person's body is developing resistance against COVID-19 infection:

- Arm discomfort
- Mild fever
- Tiredness
- Headaches
- Muscle or joint aches

Contact your healthcare provider if you notice redness or discomfort (pain) where you got the shot after 24 hours, or if side effects do not go away after a few days.

If you have an immediate severe adverse reaction to the first dosage of the COVID-19 vaccine, you should not take any more doses. When vaccines are directly responsible, severe health reactions are uncommon.

To avoid side effects, it is not recommended that you use pain killers like paracetamol before obtaining the COVID-19 vaccine. This is due to the fact that it is uncertain how painkillers may affect the vaccine's efficacy. You can use paracetamol or other pain killers if you have adverse effects such as discomfort, fever, headache, or muscle aches following vaccination.

Even after you've been vaccinated, you should continue to take precautions.

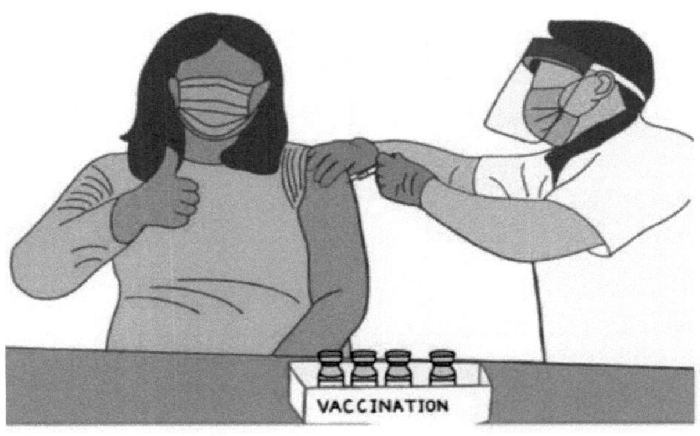

Source: pathkindlabs.com

While the COVID-19 vaccine can protect you from serious illness and death, we don't know how effective it is in preventing you from becoming infected and spreading the virus to others. The more time we give the virus to spread, the more likely it is to develop. Continue to take actions to slow and eventually stop the spread of the virus:

- Maintain a distance of at least 1 meter from other people.
- Use a mask if you're in a crowded, confined, or poorly ventilated environment.
- Frequently wash your hands
- Cover any cough or sneeze with your bent elbow while indoors with others
- Ensure proper ventilation, such as by opening a window, when indoors with others.

Source: healio.com

Every year, vaccines save millions of lives. The discovery of safe and effective COVID-19 vaccinations is a big step toward putting an end to the epidemic and getting back to doing the activities we love with the people we care about.

Taking care of everything protects us all!

References

- https://www.unicef.org/coronavirus/what-you-need-to-know-covid-vaccine
- https://www.thelancet.com/journals/lanepe/article/PIIS2666-7762(21)00258-1/fulltext
- https://www.muhealth.org/our-stories/what-are-benefits-getting-covid-19-vaccine
- http://www.google.com/search?q=importance+of+covid+vaccine&rlz=1C1DFOC enIN659IN659&oq=importance+of+covid+vaccine&aqs=chrome..
- 69i57j0i512l9.7489j0j15&sourceid=chrome&ie=UTF-8&sourceid=

  chrome&sourceid=

- https://www.who.int/emergencies/diseases/novel-coronavirus-2019/covid-19-vaccines/advice
- https://www.cdc.gov/coronavirus/2019-ncov/vaccines/vaccine-benefits.html
- https://www.pathkindlabs.com/blogs/importance-covid-19-vaccines-and-why-you-should-not-miss-i
- https://www.nature.com/articles/d41586-020-00502-w
- https://www.nejm.org/coronavirus

List Of Authors

1. History of Vaccine in India

Dr. Anshika Rajvanshi*, Dr. Shumayela Hasan**, *Sr. Asst Professor, IIMT, Asst Professor, Dept of Economics, Bhopal School of Social Sciences.*

2.COVID-19 vaccination Process and Policies in India

Krittibas Datta, *State Aided College Teacher, Department of Political Science, Jalangi Mahavidyalaya, Murshidabad, West Bengal, India.*

3. A Critical ANALYSIS OF COVID-19 vaccine Hesitancy among adolescents

Dr. ARCHANA S.S, *Assistant Professor, Mar Theophilus Training College, Nalanchira, Thiruvananthapuram, Kerala state.*

4. Importance and Relevance of Vaccine

Dr. Abhishek Srivastava, *Associate Professor, Faculty of Management Studies,* Gopal Narayan Singh University, Rohtas, Bihar.

Pranati Das, *Students, GGSIPU, Meerabai Institute of Technology, Delhi.*

5. India's Vaccine History: The March Of The Vaccines

Dr. Savita Mishra, Principal, Vidyasagar College of Education, Phansidewa, Darjeeling, West Bengal.

Divine Tomar, Pupil Teacher, Manvi Institute Of Education And Technology, SCERT.

6. Vaccine Schedule of India

Dr. Ekata Gupta, *Associate Professor, Guru Nanak Institute of Management, Delhi.*

Ayushi Sharma, *Student, BBA, GGSIPU, Delhi*

7. India's COVID-19 vaccine deployment strategies

Dr. Mukta Goyal, Principal, *Manvi Institute of Education and Technology, SCERT, Delhi.*

8.Covid-19 Vaccine: India's Plans And Deployment Strategies

Mr.Anand Prakash Dube, *Associate Professor, School of Management Sciences, Varanasi.*

Muskan Gupta, Student, *MBA (G), GGSIPU, Delhi.*

9. Covid Vaccine Challenges in Containing the Epidemic

Dr. Sridhar S, *(former)Professor, Mechanical Engineering, Channabasaveshwara Institute of Technology, Tumkur, Karnataka.*

10. Distribution Process of COVID-19 Vaccine

Dr. Anchal Pathak, *Associate Professor, Bule Hora University, Ethiopia.*

Pranati Das,*Students,GGSIPU,Meerabai Institute of Technology,Delhi.*

11. Indian Foreign Policy and COVID Vaccine

Dr. Susanta Sarkar, *Department of Political Science, Santipur College, Nadia, West Bengal.*

12. Indian Federalism and COVID Vaccines

Ms. Bulbul Sharma, Assistant Professor, P.G.Department of Political Science, D.A.V.College, Hoshiarpur.

13. Natural immunity versus vaccination immunity

Amit Kumar Verma, *Faculty,Dept of Pharmacy Rohilkhand University, Bareilly,*

Preeti Mishra, *Faculty of pharmacy, Raja Balwant Singh engineering technical campus, Agra*

Rajat Singh,[*]***Garima Kumari***[*], *B.pharma scholar,Raja Balwant Singh engineering technical campus, Agra*

14. COVID vaccines: A step toward averting the pandemic

Mrs Geetika Gulati, *Teacher Educator, Manvi Institute of Edu & Tech.,Delhi.*

Kanishka Tomar, *Pupil teacher, Manvi Institute of Education And Technology, SCERT*

15.Covid Variants: Emerging Concerns

Mr. K. C. Malik, *(Former)Associate Professor, Sri Venkateswara College, University of Delhi.*

DIVINE TOMAR, *Pupil Teacher,Manvi Institute of Education and Technology, SCERT, Delhi.*

Printed by Libri Plureos GmbH in Hamburg,
Germany